HOW TO MAKE MONEY

ANCIENT WISDOM FOR MODERN READERS

■ ■ ■ ■ ■

For a full list of titles in the series, go to https://press.princeton.edu/series/ancient-wisdom-for-modern-readers.

HOW TO MAKE MONEY

■ ■ ■ ■ ■ ■

An Ancient Guide to Wealth Management

Pliny & Co.

Selected, translated,
and introduced by Luca Grillo

PRINCETON UNIVERSITY PRESS

PRINCETON AND OXFORD

Published by Princeton University Press
41 William Street, Princeton, New Jersey 08540
99 Banbury Road, Oxford OX2 6JX

press.princeton.edu

All Rights Reserved

ISBN 9780691239125
ISBN (e-book) 9780691239132

British Library Cataloging-in-Publication Data is available

Editorial: Rob Tempio and Chloe Coy
Production Editorial: Mark Bellis
Text Design: Pamela Schnitter
Jacket Design: Heather Hansen
Production: Erin Suydam
Publicity: Tyler Hubbert and Carmen Jimenez
Copyeditor: Kathleen Kageff

Jacket Credit: Stele depicting a banker, Viminacium,
3rd century A.D. © Narodni Muzej u Beogradu

This book has been composed in Stempel Garamond LT Std

Printed on acid-free paper. ∞

Printed in the United States of America

1 3 5 7 9 10 8 6 4 2

CONTENTS

CONTENTS

INTRODUCTION

The Sabines were devastating Roman land; they even approached the city walls and besieged a Roman army led by one of the two consuls. Since the other consul seemed unable to help, the Romans opted for granting supreme power to Lucius Quintus and sent messengers to appoint him dictator. They surprised Lucius while he was digging a ditch at his family farm, but he promptly answered the call and took command of the army. In only sixteen days, he defeated the Sabines; then, having fulfilled his task, he resigned as dictator and returned to work his farm . . . or so the story goes. Of course, Lucius Quintus is better known as Cincinnatus. His legendary conduct inspired generations of Romans because it embodies some of their quintessential ideals. In him, selfless service to the state meets relentless attachment to one's farm, and the hardships of farming and fighting alike are successfully met.

About three centuries after Cincinnatus, there lived another great farmer, Marcus Porcius Cato. Cicero tells us that, just as his ancestors did, Cato would serve the state as a magistrate or soldier and then return to till his land. Someone once asked Cato about the best investment for one's estate. "Raising cattle successfully," he replied. "And what comes second?" "Raising them well enough." "And third?" "Raising them poorly." "And fourth?" "Cultivating land." "But"—added the interlocutor—"what about moneylending?" to which Cato replied, "And what about murdering someone?" (Cicero, *On Duties* [*De officiis*], bk. 2, chap. 89).[1]

When it came to livelihood, Romans had strong views, but perhaps they all agreed on one point: there is no greater occupation than farming. Indeed, the Roman economy, being typically premodern, was dominated by agriculture. And yet when Cicero praised Cato for presenting agriculture as the most profitable, enjoyable, and dignified job, he was not thinking about the type of farming Cincinnatus did. It is one thing to supervise one's estates from a horse or a litter, and one another to get one's hands dirty and actually till the land. Whether or not Cincinnatus personally dug his ditches, his myth exemplifies an ideal that leading Romans continued to hold even when it became increasingly divorced from their actual life. Indeed, Romans idealized farming and service to the state as the best occupations and looked with suspicion, or even contempt, at other ventures, however lucrative. Yet these strong views were only part of the story. In real life, service was not always as selfless as Cincinnatus's was; and over time, various professions, including moneylending, flourished aside from raising cattle and farming, pace Cato.

We can start making sense of how Romans earned a living, then, by appreciating a few tenets, which may feel more or less familiar to us. First off, the most respected and the most lucrative occupations did not necessarily coincide. For this reason, as we tour some of the numerous ways to make money in ancient Rome, we can examine how individuals creatively navigated the gap between profit and respectability.

As one would expect, this gap led Romans to hold quite different views on the several professions, and we need to respect these differences, even when it amounts to allowing that contradictory attitudes co-existed. For example, Cicero distinguished between dignified and demeaning jobs. Agriculture is of course the most desirable occupation, while professions such as usury and tax collection lie at the bottom, because they elicit popular hatred. Similarly, any form of waged labor is servile, because "the very wage is like a bond of slavery" (Cicero, *On Duties* [*De officiis*], bk. 1, chap. 150);[2] craftsmen engage in demeaning trades as well, and for the most part merchants do the same. Occupations such as medicine, architecture, and teaching lay somewhere in between; on the one hand, they raise above the most demeaning jobs because they engage the mind and benefit the community; on the other hand, they do not fully suit the elite, being "respectable for individuals whose social class they befit." In fact, more often than not, doctors and teachers in ancient Rome were slaves or freedmen, but Cicero ranks their profession above that of tax collectors and craftsmen, who were often born free.

Cicero documents the view of the male elite, and this view documents a mismatch between economic profitability, moral respectability, and social class. It also documents a mismatch with different, and perhaps statistically more prominent, points of view. For example, contrary to the elitist perspective expressed by Cicero, plenty of inscriptions demonstrate that merchants and craftsmen took pride in what they did. They could sign their products, join in associations with colleagues involved in the same craft, sponsor events for the community, and publicly support local candidates. Graffiti from Pompeii suggest that individuals proudly identified themselves with their job and that, by joining their craft association, they found a way to fulfill the Roman ideal of service and to contribute to the *res publica*, that is, to the state. For example, certain inscriptions read "the chicken sellers invite you to vote for Epidius and Suettius," "the mat makers ask you to elect Lollius," "the grocery sellers ask you to support Marcus Priscus," and "the bakers urge you to elect Trebius," and the list goes on.[3] And yet, the Roman elite typically looked down on such occupations. Some 150 years after Cicero, a poet named Martial even poked fun at some artisans' aspiration to partake in the civic life of towns such as Bologna and Modena: "Educated Bologna, a cobbler who repairs shoes offered some games for you; a wool fuller did the same for you, Modena. Now, where is the innkeeper going to offer the next games?" (Martial, *Epigrams*, bk. 3, epigram 59).[4]

Another tenet of Roman ways of making a living, then, is that some very common jobs, being despised by the elite, are often underdocumented or completely overlooked by literary sources. To appreciate the work of female, middle- and lower-class individuals, we must turn to graffiti, such as the ones found in Pompeii, and to inscriptions, especially epitaphs carved on tombstones. Epitaphs vary dramatically: the wealthy, who could afford costly funerals and tombs, often recorded their life and achievements in some detail. More typically, however, epitaphs briefly commemorate the deceased by recording their name and, at times, by adding a few words about their family, age, occupation, and possibly more. For this reason, the following chapters place excerpts from literary sources alongside bits of information taken from Latin inscriptions. But we should not forget that a great number of Romans were buried anonymously in common graves, so that their lives and work lay beyond our reach. Indeed, it has been calculated that a cheap epitaph cost the equivalent of three months' wages for an unskilled laborer. Thus, epitaphs allow us to broaden our grasp of Roman ways to make a living beyond the narrow viewpoint of the male elite. Be that as it may, our point of view remains narrow.

Roman society was sexist and hierarchical. For example, a very typical formula on epitaphs commemorating deceased females reads "she kept an eye over the house, she spun wool."[5] This common phrasing provides little information about the deceased, being basically a synonym for "she was a good woman," and hence expressing and reinforcing a social expectation. And yet, Roman society allowed for some surprising mobility, as well, especially by the standards of the ancient Mediterranean. For example, epitaphs tell stories of successful slaves and women. Publius Decimius Eros Merula used to be a slave doctor from Assisi; he bought his freedom, spent even more in support of his local community, and left a considerable estate. Similarly, a funeral monument outside of Pompeii commemorates a freedwoman called Naevoleia. The monument includes an enclosure with various niches for burying Naevoleia and members of her household; on top of the enclosure an altar with sculptural reliefs represents a ship, among other figures, and an honorific chair. The ship must suggest that she made her fortune thanks to overseas commerce, and the chair commemorates an honor bestowed on her husband. Remarkably, her husband erected a tomb as well, to share with his wife, but Naevoleia must have felt unsatisfied, and so she had another and more elaborate tomb built. The inscription both acknowledges and surpasses her husband. To be sure, there was no class and gender equality, but stories like Publius Decimius's and Naevoleia's demonstrate that slaves and women could become financially successful and celebrate their achievements with pride.

The elite rarely shared that pride, but Romans could question their own idealization of various occupations, including farming. A generation after Cicero, Horace ironically captured the widespread glorification of country life: "lucky is the one who, removed from the cares of city business, plows the estate he inherited from his fathers; lucky is the one who attends cattle, shears sheep, prunes trees, picks pears and grapes, and enjoys peaceful sleep at the murmur of running streams."[6] This lavish praise of farming and idyllic portrayal of country life goes on for sixty-six lines, until the readers have a startling surprise: "thus spoke Alfius, the moneylender, who's just about to become a farmer, then he cashed in all the money he lent out, and he lent it out again."

Horace demonstrates that, while being dominated by agriculture (the subject of chapter 1), the Roman economy and psyche embraced other ways to make money as well. With chapters 2 and 3, we abandon the countryside to meet the Romans in the marketplace, in towns and provinces, where some people made a living through taxation or through public contracts. This encounter throws up similarities to our world: they had companies, with CEOs, employees, and shareholders; they crafted detailed contracts, regulated by meticulous laws, which took into account investment risks. They enjoyed a relatively open society, where talented individuals could start out from the bottom, even as slaves, buy themselves off, continue to invest successfully, and become billionaires. This openness was a source of pride for some and a source of concern for some others.

Whatever their attitude, Romans liked money and the power that comes with it. For example, Trimalchio bragged about his wealth; Seneca accumulated a huge fortune but taught that wealth does not buy one's happiness; and Eumachia inherited a successful brick factory from her father. Having married well and outlived her husband, she used her money and influence to engage in philanthropy. In other words, some looked at their financial dealings as a measure of their worth, and some preached moderation in reaping interests, while some others, having made millions, took pleasure in giving back to the broader community.

Giving back to the community was a means to express gratitude for the people's support and to secure yet more support for the future. Ambitious politicians would even incur debt in order to sponsor lavish gladiatorial games and other spectacles to entertain the masses. Chapters 4 and 5 show how such investments in popularity, which were unquestionably expensive, could win or lose one's fortune and reputation. Military campaigns could meet the same fate and bolster or ruin one's profit and respectability.

Perhaps elites, such as Cato and Cicero, and non-elites, such as Merula and Naevoleia, agreed that profit and respectability did not always go hand in hand. Chapter 6 shows that the gap between economic and social rewards is nowhere more evident than in human trafficking. Dealing slaves and managing prostitutes (or gladiators) was unquestionably legal, lucrative, and despised. For this reason, the elite often engaged in such activities through go-betweens, thus cashing in the money while saving face.

Clearly, the Roman world presents many similarities to our own, but these similarities should not blind us to one more tenet of Roman ways to make money. For centuries, the Roman economy was primitive. The Romans had conquered an empire by the end of the third century BCE, *before* developing a money economy and a political structure capable of sustaining it. Hence, to mention but one example, they forged a terrible system of taxation, as shown in chapter 3. Eventually they caught up with the realization that Rome was no longer a city-state but the capital of an empire. But this bartering delay left its mark on the later mind-set and vocabulary. To pay soldiers and workers they used to weigh (*pendo*) a wage (*stips*), a process called *stipendium*. Workers could be compensated also with a *munus* (hence, "remuneration"), which originally indicated a "gift" or payment in kind.

The Roman mint was related to a temple dedicated to Juno Moneta, and around the time of Augustus and of Jesus some poets started to use *moneta* as shorthand for "money." The main Latin word for money, however, remained *pecunia*, which comes from *pecus*, "cattle," and which brings us back full circle to Cato's ideal method of investing. For the Romans money is cattle. English derivatives can be revealing and misleading at once: to us "pecuniary remuneration" is elegant for "money, please," while to the Romans it signified cattle, a common currency, but one you can't put in your pocket and take to the currency exchange.

Unfortunately, we have no single ancient treatise about Roman ways to make money, and I suspect that if we did, it would take for granted much of what we may want to know. Fortunately, however, institutions, mind-sets, and vocabulary, both sophisticated and backward, disseminated various hints. *How to Make Money* is a collection of texts, which, like fossils, reveal traces of life crystallized from a different era. If we crack these fossils open we can encounter this different era on its own terms, and in turn this encounter may reveal many unexpected differences and similarities to our world.

In accordance with the intent of the series, this book will present ancient wisdom to modern readers by allowing a variety of classical texts to speak for themselves. However, it cannot even attempt to give a full picture of Roman occupations. For example, high mortality made will hunting widespread; poverty and spotty control made theft and robbery quite common; and gambling was highly popular. These ways to make (or lose) money left a mark in official documents and in Latin literature, especially in comedies and in novels, but they lay outside the scope of this book. As you read, you will encounter some ancient methods of making capital grow through no medium beyond the strong opinions of the Romans themselves. What were the risks and rewards of different jobs? And how did various occupations rank in the social and ethical imaginary of elite and nonelite Romans?

HOW TO MAKE MONEY

Chapter 1

HOW TO BECOME RICH, ENVIED, AND RESPECTED

Farming

Introduction

In the third century BCE, two main powers coexisted in the western Mediterranean: Rome and Carthage. Eventually they clashed. Thanks to the military genius of Hannibal, Carthage came very close to winning the war; in the end, however, Rome triumphed. Ancient and modern historians agree that the contenders had comparable resources and power, and yet they were radically different. Carthage had developed a maritime and commercial empire; it mostly cared about keeping control over some ports strategic for safeguarding its trade network in the Mediterranean. As a result, when it came to war, Carthage heavily relied on its fleet and employed mercenaries. The Roman economy, on the other hand, was neither commercial nor industrial, but agricultural. Accordingly, Rome relied mainly on its infantry, and the core of its army was made up of farmers who fought to defend their land.

FARMING

In many ways, the outcome of the Second Punic War transformed the Roman economy, but it did not alter its nature. Rome remained grounded in agriculture. Indeed, upon defeating Carthage, Romans, not content with their new acquisition of strategic ports, actually created two new provinces: Sardinia and Sicily. In other words, farmers wanted more land.

Indeed, in return for their service, soldiers could expect a stipend and special rewards, which mostly depended on their rank in the army and on the success and generosity of a general. The highest reward was a plot of land. This plot typically was part of some freshly conquered territory, though some plots were located in reclaimed land or in newly established colonies. Florence, Bologna, Cologne (meaning "the colony"), York, and Lyon owe their origin or their growth to settlements of land-hungry veterans.

It would be hard to overstate the central position that agriculture occupied in the Roman psyche. As mentioned in the introduction, *pecunia* is Latin for "cattle" and hence for "money"; similarly, *laetus* means "well-manured" or "fertile" and hence "joyful," while *felix*, which means "fruitful," came to mean "lucky." If money is cattle, then being happy and blessed means having a well-manured field that bears fruit. Being a good farmer, then, was about more than achieving financial success. One can begin to see why the Romans reinvested in land the profit they had acquired through war and commerce.

Clearly, the centrality of agriculture in the Roman imagination, economy, and language can reveal a lot about the ways they earned a living, with implications that reach beyond agriculture. For one thing, it means that, however idealized, the story of Cincinnatus, who went from being a farmer to being a dictator and then back to a farmer, captures an unquestionably historical truth. Not only did Rome and the majesty of its empire grow directly out of an initially marginal and irrelevant peasant society, but even after Rome had become the leading economy in the Mediterranean, farming and agriculture remained the ideal and the measure of individual success. The first two selections of this chapter portray the endurance of the agricultural ideal and its adaptation to an economy that grew over the centuries. The next two selections reveal some secrets for succeeding in agriculture, or in other words, they show how to become rich, joyful, and blessed. For all this bounty, however, we cannot forget that, as Rome expanded its borders, slaves labored long hours in the fields, while the elite reaped the benefit of their work. The last passage, a short fragment from an epitaph, gives a voice to those enslaved and often invisible laborers.

Texts 1 and 2. Introduction: How to Choose a Farm

When the envoys from the Roman senate reached Cincinnatus, they found him working his land, and Livy specifies that he owned four acres. This may well be another piece of historical information. At the time of Cincinnatus (fifth century BCE), the Roman territory was as big as Delaware and looked like a quilt of small family farms. Typically, farmers passed on to their descendants their land and their dream: to work a few acres, produce enough to support a family, and then pass it down to the next generation. Truly, the fifth century proved particularly challenging for the Romans, but it taught them to defend ferociously their plot of land. After rejecting the Etruscan kings (traditionally in 509 BCE), the budding Roman Republic was besieged by enemies on all sides. Its economy was in desperate shape, with disruptions in trade and several crop failures. Besides, a series of epidemics hit, while civil unrest further challenged the survival of Rome.

Fighting against the odds for a couple of centuries, Rome established itself as the main power in central Italy. Then, after defeating Carthage, Romans safely controlled the western Mediterranean. In 218, when the Second Punic War broke out, Cato was about sixteen years old, and by the time he died in 149 BCE, he had witnessed a radical growth in the Roman economy. In many ways, his life must have been easier than Cincinnatus's. Cato, however, faced a problem that Cincinnatus never had. Cato needed to assess the quality of *more* land for sale. Perhaps, other Romans of his time nourished similar aspirations, because Cato begins his treatise *On Agriculture* with advice on choosing good land.

What's the point of teaching agriculture to an audience of farmers? The type of farm Cato had in mind was quite different from what Cincinnatus and generations of Romans used to own. Starting from the Second Punic War, overseas conquests brought in more land and slaves. Cato envisioned a unit of about twenty-five acres, and much of his treatise dealt with something unfamiliar to farmers of earlier generations, such as the management of laborers and slaves and the supervision of their work.

Cato dedicated *On Agriculture* to his son, but he had a larger audience in mind—an audience that now includes us. This treatise is the earliest piece of Latin prose we have. The grammar is archaic, the syntax and style repetitive and bare, the tone straightforward, top-down, and preachy. All in all, although some recommendations may seem banal, Cato's precepts offer precious insights into a world that, though changing, remained centered on agriculture.

Two and half centuries later, another senator, Younger Pliny (61–113 CE), was equally interested in agriculture, and indeed he wrestled with the same problem that Cato had. In a letter to a friend, he openly disclosed his aspirations and reservations about buying more land. Just like Cato, Pliny did not write for his addressee only; he published his letters to reach a broader audience and posed as a member of the Roman elite dealing with an elite problem—the purchase of new farmland.

In facing a possible acquisition, Cato and Pliny seem to go through a strikingly similar checklist, but their style and tone could not be more different. Pliny's polished Latin, smooth grammar, and amicable manner reflect not only his different personality but also the fashions of his time. By the end of the first century CE, Rome was the capital of a well-established and flourishing empire and had developed a robust body of first-class literature. Pliny's letters reflect these literary developments.

Similarly, the content of Pliny's letter documents the massive economic growth that had intervened since the time of Cato. The estate Pliny had in mind was as different from Cato's twenty-five-acre farm as Cato's was from Cincinnatus's. The larger size of the estate and the fact that this larger estate was only one of the many that Pliny owned demanded a more complex staff. Unsurprisingly, then, Pliny contemplated the necessity of employing more specialized workers, such as gardeners, stewards, and tenants. Stewards, *atrienses*, took their name from the *atrium*, the center of a countryside villa. They lived in the villa and supervised the administration of an estate when the owner was gone, which was most of the time. Tenants, *coloni*, were mostly free people who rented some land and worked it for a fee to the owner. Typically, tenants pledged some security for renting farmland, and since they tended to have little extra cash, often the best thing they could pledge were their very farming tools. If there was a bad year and they fell in arrears, landowners could then take their tools. Doing so, however, could backfire for a landowner, as a paucity of workers might force him to look for new tenants or to buy more slaves, lest his land lie fallow.

Quo modo agrum emi pararique oporteat.

Praedium quom parare cogitabis, sic in animo habeto: uti ne cupide emas neve opera tua parcas visere et ne satis habeas semel circumire; quotiens ibis, totiens magis placebit quod bonum erit. Vicini quo pacto niteant, id animum advertito: in bona regione bene nitere oportebit. Et uti eo introeas et circumspicias, uti inde exire possis. Uti bonum caelum habeat; ne calamitosum siet; solo bono, sua virtute valeat. Si poteris, sub radice montis siet, in meridiem spectet, loco salubri; operariorum copia siet, bonumque aquarium, oppidum validum prope siet; aut mare aut amnis, qua naves ambulant, aut via bona celerisque. Siet in his agris qui non saepe dominum mutant: qui in his agris praedia vendiderint, eos pigeat vendidisse.

Uti bene aedificatum siet. Caveto alienam disciplinam temere contemnas. De domino bono bonoque aedificatore melius emetur. Ad villam cum venies, videto vasa torcula et dolia multane sient: ubi non erunt, scito pro ratione fructum esse. Instrumenti ne

1. HOW TO CHOOSE A FARM, ELDER CATO, ON AGRICULTURE (DE AGRICULTURA) 1

How to Buy and Prepare Land

Here's what you need to keep in mind when you're thinking of purchasing a lot of land. Don't be emotional; don't refrain from careful examination; don't be satisfied with one tour of the property. If the lot is a good one, the more you visit it, the more you'll like it. Pay attention to the neighbors: are they thriving? Thriving neighbors prove that the land is good. Consider the entrance to the land but also the exit. Make sure that it has a good rather than bad climate, and that it is fertile and naturally rich. Ideally, find land at the foot of a mountain, facing south, and in the right position. Make sure that there are many day laborers and a natural reserve of water close by, and that it borders a prosperous town, or the sea or a river, so that access by water or land is quick and easy. A high turnover of ownership is a bad sign; and if someone sells property, let him regret it.

Check how solid the buildings are, and don't hastily judge what the neighbors built. It's better to buy from an owner who's also a good builder. When you enter the country house, check the number of presses and storing jars: finding few suggests that the harvest is scarce. There should not be too many farming tools. Also make sure that the land is in a good location. Make sure that there are no more tools than necessary

magni siet, [loco bono siet]. Videto quam minimi instrumenti sumptuosusque ager ne siet. Scito idem agrum quod hominem, quamvis quaestuosus siet, si sumptuosus erit, relinqui non multum. Praedium quod primum siet, si me rogabis, sic dicam: de omnibus agris optimoque loco iugera agri centum, vinea est prima, vel si vino multo est; secundo loco hortus irriguus; tertio salictum; quarto oletum; quinto pratum; sexto campus frumentarius; septimo silva caedua; octavo arbustum; nono glandaria silva.

C. PLINIUS CALVISIO RUFO SUO S.

Assumo te in consilium rei familiaris, ut soleo. Praedia agris meis vicina atque etiam inserta venalia sunt. In his me multa sollicitant, aliqua nec minora deterrent. Sollicitat primum ipsa pulchritudo iungendi; deinde, quod non minus utile quam voluptuosum, posse utraque eadem opera eodem viatico invisere, sub eodem procuratore ac paene isdem actoribus habere, unam villam colere et ornare, alteram tantum tueri. Inest huic computationi sumptus supellectilis, sumptus atriensium topiariorum fabrorum atque etiam venatorii instrumenti; quae plurimum refert unum in locum conferas an in diversa dispergas. Contra vereor

and that the land won't incur extra costs. Remember that fields are just like people: if they produce but cost too much, there's not much profit. If you ask me what the best farm is, this is what I would say: of all fields located in an ideal location, go for a plot of twenty-five acres. Vines should occupy the best location, especially if they produce much wine, and a well-watered garden takes the second best; plots of willows and of olive trees take the third and fourth; the fifth goes to a meadow, the sixth to a grain field; the seventh, eighth, and ninth go to trees that produce wood, fruit, and acorns.

2. TO BUY OR NOT TO BUY, YOUNGER PLINY, LETTERS (EPISTULARUM LIBER) III 19

Pliny Sends Greetings to His Dear Calvisius Rufus

As per usual, I need you to advise me about some family business matters. An estate next to my fields—in fact it cuts into mine—is up for sale. I'm very intrigued, but there are also some significant deterrents. First off, I'm tempted by the very nice prospect of joining the two properties, then by how convenient and pleasant it would be to visit both lands with one journey and to place both under the same manager. It would be practical for me to have the same staff and to inhabit and furnish one country house, while just keeping the other one in good shape. Part of my calculations are also the costs of furnishing;

ne sit incautum, rem tam magnam isdem tempestatibus isdem casibus subdere; tutius videtur incerta fortunae possessionum varietatibus experiri. Habet etiam multum iucunditatis soli caelique mutatio, ipsaque illa peregrinatio inter sua. Iam, quod deliberationis nostrae caput est, agri sunt fertiles pingues aquosi; constant campis vineis silvis, quae materiam et ex ea reditum sicut modicum ita statum praestant. Sed haec felicitas terrae imbecillis cultoribus fatigatur. Nam possessor prior saepius vendidit pignora, et dum reliqua colonorum minuit ad tempus, vires in posterum exhausit, quarum defectione rursus reliqua creverunt. Sunt ergo instruendi eo pluris quod frugi mancipiis; nam nec ipse usquam vinctos habeo nec ibi quisquam.

Superest ut scias quanti videantur posse emi. Sestertio triciens, non quia non aliquando quinquagiens fuerint, verum et hac penuria colonorum et communi temporis iniquitate ut reditus agrorum sic etiam pretium retro abiit. Quaeris an hoc ipsum triciens facile

the expense for stewards, gardeners, and handy-men; not to mention hunting gear and whether it is collected in one place or scattered in many, which makes a big difference. But on the other hand, I worry that subjecting such a huge property to the risks of the same weather may not be sensible. It seems safer to undergo fortune's uncertainties with separate properties. Moreover, it's always pleasant to change location and air and to travel from one's own estate to the next. So the key point in my reasoning is that the land is fertile, rich, and well watered; the property consists of fields, vineyards, and trees that produce wood—a modest but secure source of income. But this fertility is compromised by the scarcity of workers, because the previous owner too often sold the tools that the tenants had pledged. In this way he reduced their debt for a while, but in the long term he drained their resources, and for this reason the arrears have picked up again. As a result, it needs to be replenished with slaves and at greater expense because they have to be reliable, given that neither I nor anyone else there keeps them in chains.

There's one last thing you need to know—the sale price. They want 3 million sestertii; they used to ask for 5, but because of the scarcity of farmers and the current crisis, the revenue and the price of land have gone down all at once. You may wonder if I can easily come up with that 3 million; I have invested almost entirely in estates, but I have some money on hand

colligere possimus. Sum quidem prope totus in prae-
diis, aliquid tamen fenero, nec molestum erit mutuari;
accipiam a socru, cuius arca non secus ac mea utor. Pro-
inde hoc te non moveat, si cetera non refragantur, quae
velim quam diligentissime examines. Nam cum in omnibus rebus tum in disponendis facultatibus plurimum
tibi et usus et providentiae superest. Vale.

from interest, and I can take out a loan without a problem. I plan to borrow from my mother-in-law, whose account I can access as easily as my own. So do not worry about me securing the money, if you have no objections to the other considerations, which I'd ask you, please, to ponder as carefully as possible. For I know that you have experience and wisdom in every matter and especially in managing properties. Be well.

Texts 3 and 4. Introduction: How to Optimize Land Production

Once farmers or landlords secured a plot of land, they had to make it productive. In the early centuries of the Roman Republic, when the economy relied on small subsistence farmers à la Cincinnatus, deciding what to grow and knowing how to do it was a matter of life or death. Choosing wisely meant the difference between managing and failing to support a family. For example, growing vines or olive trees was no doubt more lucrative than growing vegetables, but not everyone could afford the investment. It takes some years for a vineyard or for olive trees to bear fruit, and some farmers were in no position to wait. Those who made the investment, however, in order to make the most of their small plot, had to know how densely they could plant and how quickly they could grow vines, especially because hastening growth could backfire in the long run. The same principle applies to producing and aging wine. Similarly, allotting some land to trees that generate only wood is less profitable than growing vegetables, but it is also safer, in case hail or some other natural calamity should strike, and a year of bad crops should ensue. For this reason, at the end of the first selection, Cato advised his son to diversify and grow nine different types of produce. Of course, such diversification is more easily achieved on a twenty-five-acre than on a four-acre farmstead.

The next set of selections deals with recommendations about growing vines and selling wine. They are taken from the Elder Pliny's *Natural History*. Elder Pliny (23–79 CE) was the adoptive uncle of Younger Pliny (whom we met in selection 2). He is most known for his works and manner of death. An incredibly prolific and versatile author, he wrote about history, biology, grammar, astronomy, geography, medicine, mineralogy, and the arts, among other subjects. His *Natural History*, in thirty-seven books, documents the range of his interests and reveals much about Roman scientific knowledge: diamonds are so hard that if put on an anvil and struck with the hammer, they shatter the hammer, unless they are drenched in fresh and warm goat blood; lightning strikes are fires falling on earth from the planets; and the shape and color of many plants resemble the part of the body they have the power to cure.

Today, Elder Pliny's encyclopedic knowledge may look like encyclopedic ignorance. But tellingly, when dealing with agriculture, Pliny came much closer to the mark, as he relied on hard-won knowledge from centuries of subsistence farming. Much of what he taught about growing vines closely resembles practices still recommended on the websites of various American universities. Cut pieces of roots, also known as "rooted cuttings," or sprouts can be used to form new shoots; and buds (or "eyes," as Pliny names them) must be pruned at specific times. One may add that

Pliny's theories, even when inaccurate or abstruse, proved influential. For example, he is rightly regarded as one of the founding fathers of the so-called doctrine of signatures, the theory that connects a plant's look to its medical power. A present-day nephrologist would not prescribe a plant for kidney stones, but the plant that Pliny recommended for this malady is to this day called "stone-crop" or "gromwell." Powdered stone-crop/gromwell root is still thought to have curative powers, and a $25 package gets glowing reviews on Amazon.

The range of Elder Pliny's interests bears witness to a genuine curiosity, which his nephew, Younger Pliny, immortalized in a letter. When Mount Vesuvius erupted in 79 CE, both Elder and Younger Pliny happened to be at the Bay of Naples, and "as a real scholar, my uncle realized that the eruption demanded closer scrutiny and called for a boat."[7] His sense of duty prevailed, so he set out to rescue other people, until he died by suffocating on ashes and gas.

Pliny sprinkled his *Natural History* with many short and entertaining stories and anecdotes, such as that of Caius Furius Cresimus (selection 4). Acquiring some land, deciding what to grow, and knowing how to do it was still not enough. A successful farmer had to take good care of his tools as well. For the Romans, farmers possessed three types of tools: tools that do not move and do not speak, like ploughs and shovels; tools that move but do not speak, like donkeys and oxen; and "tools" that move and speak, like slaves. Selection 4 tells the story of a former slave who became a farmer and was summoned to court. He had to appear in front of the Roman tribal assembly, which typically judged trials concerning noncapital cases. By the time Cresimus appeared in court, he was already wealthy and envied, but only his treatment of his "tools" made him respected as well. Many and noble individuals strove to fulfill the ideal of the Roman farmer: Cincinnatus became dictator; Elder Cato became censor; Elder Pliny was an all-rounder, and his nephew a senator and first-rank writer. Each taught us much about agriculture. But no one incarnates this ideal better than Caius Furius Cresimus, a former slave.

Interesse medio temperamento inter binas vites oportet pedes quinos, minimum autem laeto solo pedes
quaternos, tenui plurimum octonos—Umbri et Marsi
ad vicenos intermittunt arationis gratia in his, quae vocant porculeta—, pluvio et caliginoso tractu rariores
poni, sicco densiores. subtilitas parsimoniae conpen-
dia invenit, cum vinea in pastinato seratur, obiter
seminarium faciendi, ut et viveradix loco suo et mal-
leolus, qui transferatur, inter vites et ordines seratur,
quae ratio in iugero circiter XVI viveradicum donat.
Interest autem biennium fructus quo tardius in sato
provenit quam in tralato. Viveradix posita in vinea
post annum resecatur usque ad terram, ut unus tantum emineat oculus, adminiculo iuxta adfixo et fimo
addito. Simili modo et secundo anno reciditur vir-
esque concipit <e>t intra se pascit suffecturas oneri.
Alias festinatione pariendi gracilis atque eiuncida, ni
cohibeatur castigatione tali, in fetum exeat tota.
Nihil avidius nascitur ac, nisi ad pariendum vires serventur, tota fit fetus.

3A. VINICULTURE AND WINE PRODUCTION, ELDER PLINY, NATURAL HISTORY (NATURALIS HISTORIA) XVII 171–73

The gap between two rows of vines must measure five feet on average, with a minimum of four, when the soil is fertile, and a maximum of eight, when it is poor. Umbrians and Marsians leave up to twenty feet to plow the strip of land between, which they call *fertile strips*. A wet and foggy climate calls for more spacing, but rows can be closer in dry weather. Pressure to save time has led to some profitable discoveries. At the time when a vine is planted in a plowed row, take care to nourish young plants as well. Rooted cuttings must be implanted in their permanent place, and the sprouts, which will later be uprooted, must be planted in the space between vine rows. This trick yields about sixteen thousand rooted cuttings per acre. One gains two years of production, since what is planted from scratch bears fruit slower than what is transplanted. One year later, the rooted cuttings placed among the vines are cut to the ground, so that only an eye sticks out; one must add a support next to it and some fertilizer. This eye is cut in the same way on the following year as well, so that it gains strength and nourishment for what's needed to produce fruit. Otherwise, hastening to produce, it becomes slender and meager, and, if it is not constrained by drastic intervention, it gets completely consumed in the first growth. There's nothing

Tertius vineae annus palmitem velocem robustumque emittit et quem faciat aetas vitem. Hic in iugum insilit. Aliqui tum excaecant eum supina falce auferendo oculos, ut longius evocent, noxia iniuria. Utilior enim consuetudo pariendi satiusque pampinos adiugatae detergere usque quo placeat roborari eam. Sunt qui vetant tangi proximo anno, quam tralata sit, neque ante LX mensem falce curari, tunc autem ad III gemmas recidi. Alii et proximo quidem anno recidunt, sed ut ternos quaternosve singulis annis adiciant articulos, quarto demum perducant ad iugum. Id utrimque fructu tardum, praeterea retorridum et nodosum pumilionum increment. Optimum autem matrem esse firmam, postea fetum audacem. Nec tutum est quod cicatricosum, magno imperitiae errore; quidquid est tale, plagis nascitur, non e matre. Totas habeat illa vires, dum roboratur, et annuos accipiet tota fetus, cum permissum fuerit nasci. Nihil natura portionibus parit. Quae excreverit satis firma, protinus in iugo collocari debebit; si etiamnum infirmior erit, sub ipso iugo hospitari recisa. Viribus, non aetate, decernitur. Temerarium est ante crassitudinem pollicarem viti imperare.

that grows faster, to the point that, if energy is not spared for bearing fruit, a vine gets entirely consumed by its first growth.

3B. VINICULTURE AND WINE PRODUCTION, ELDER PLINY, NATURAL HISTORY (NATURALIS HISTORIA) XVII 175–78

In its third year, the vine produces a strong shoot that grows quickly and in time turns into the vine itself. This mounts itself to the horizontal bar. Some farmers blind it by cutting off its eyes with the back side of a sickle. They think it helps it to grow longer, but this is in fact harmful. For it is more helpful that a vine get used to bearing fruit; and removing its foliage when it is on the bar until one feels it is sufficiently strong is more than enough. Some don't touch it for one year after it has been transplanted and don't prune it with a sickle for sixty months; at this point they recommend cutting off the buds, leaving only three per vine. Others cut it instead in the year following their transplant as well, but in such a way as to let them produce three or four knots per year, and finally, in the fourth year, they let it reach the bar. In either case, the vine thus treated becomes slow in bearing fruit, as well as being more wrinkled and knottier, with a growth typical of dwarf plants. It is best when a vine has a solid mother trunk, and then the shoots grow boldly. But what bears scars remains weak, and wounding a vine is a big mistake typical of inexperience.

Sequente anno palmites educentur pro viribus matris. Singuli aut gemini. Iidem et secuto, si coget infirmitas, nutriantur, tertioque demum II adiciantur. Nec sunt plures quaternis umquam permittendi, breviterque non indulgendum et semper inhibenda fecunditas est. Ea est natura, ut parere malit quam vivere. Quidquid materiae adimitur, fructui accedit. Illa semina mavult quam fructum gigni, quoniam fructus caduca res. Sic perniciose luxuriat, nec ampliat se, se egerit.

What grows in this case is not born from the core, but from the wounds. Let a vine retain all its energy when it needs to build up strength, and let the entire vine keep its shoots every year, when they are allowed to spring forth. For nature generates nothing in disjointed segments. A vine that has grown sturdy enough will be carefully and promptly placed on the bar; if it is still too weak, it needs to be pruned and find shelter under the bar; this depends on its strength, not on its age, and demanding anything from a vine before it reaches the diameter of a thumb is risky. The next year, let it grow one or two arms in proportion to the strength of its trunk. If weakness gets in the way, let the vine just nourish the same arms for the following year, but add two more on the third. You should never let it grow more than four per year. In short, do not yield to a vine's exuberance, but always keep it in check. This plant has the following nature: it prefers to give birth than to stay alive. But whatever you take away from the wood goes into the fruit. The vine prefers to produce shoots above fruit, because fruit perishes. In other words, the vine swells destructively: it does not gain strength but drives its own life out.

in reliquis claritas generi non fuit alicui: anno fuit omnium generum bonitate L. Opimio cos., cum C. Gracchus tri<bunus> pl<ebem> seditionibus agitans est interemptus. Ea caeli temperies fulsit (cocturam vocant) solis opere natali urbis DCXXXIII, durantque adhuc vin<a> ea ducentis fere annis, iam in speciem redacta mellis asperi—etenim haec natura vinis in vetustate est—, nec potari per se queant pervincive aqua, usque in amaritudinem carie indomita; sed ceteris vinis commendandis minima aliqua mixtura medicamenta sunt. Quod ut eius temporis aestimatione in singulas amphoras centeni nummi statuantur, ex his tan<tu>m usura multiplicata semissibus, quae civilis ac modica est, in C. Caesaris Germanici fili principatu anno CLX singulas uncias vini constitisse, nobili exemplo docuimus referentes vitam Pomponii Secundi vatis cenamque quam principi illi dedit. Tantum pecuniarum detinent apothecae! nec alia res maius incrementum sentit ad vicensimum annum maiusve ab eo dispendium, non proficiente pretio; raro quippe adhuc fuere, nec nisi in nepotatu, singulis testis milia nummum.

3C. AGING AND SELLING WINE, ELDER PLINY, NATURAL HISTORY (NATURALIS HISTORIA) XIV 55–57

None of the other wines won fame. But one year the quality of every wine was off the chart, when L. Opimius was consul and the tribune Gaius Gracchus was killed for agitating seditions of the plebs. In the year 633 from the foundation of Rome [121 BCE] the climate was so warm, thanks to the hot sun (a phenomenon known as "grape boiling"), that wines of that year are stored up to this day, almost two centuries later; they turned into a sort of bitter honey, for such is the nature of aged wine, and it cannot be drunk pure or diluted with water, because they went indigestibly flat and taste bitter. Small portions of these aged wines, however, are suitable for cutting to ennoble other wines. Let's say that with the rate of appreciation of that time, each amphora costs 100 sestertii; on top of this, put a 6 percent increase of interest per year, which is lawful and moderate. After 160 years, when Gaius Caesar, the son of Germanicus was emperor [in 40 CE, under the rule of Gaius, better known as Caligula], the price for an ounce of this wine was fixed, as I have shown with a famous example about the poet Pomponius Secundus and the dinner he offered to the emperor. Cellars can yield this much money! Nothing else reaps comparable interest for the first twenty years but also suffers greater devaluation afterward; this is because, after twenty years, the price stops growing. Up to now, indeed, it has happened only occasionally (and never without some extravagance) that a jug went for 1,000 sestertii.

Nequeo mihi temperare, quo minus unum exemplum antiquitatis adferam, ex quo intellegi possit, apud populum etiam de culturis agendi morem fuisse qualiterque defendi soliti sint illi viri. C. Furius Cresimus e servitute liberatus admodum agello largiores multo fructus perciperet, quam ex amplissimis vicinitas, in invidia erat magna, ceu fruges alienas perliceret veneficiis. Quamobrem ab Spurio Albino curuli aedile die dicta metuens damnationem, cum in suffragium tribus oporteret ire, instrumentum rusticum omne in forum attulit et adduxit familiam suam validam atque, ut ait Piso, bene curatam ac vestitam, ferramenta egregie facta, graves ligones, vomeres ponderosos, boves saturos. Postea dixit: "Veneficia mea, Quirites, haec sunt, nec possum vobis ostendere aut in forum adducere lucubrationes meas vigiliasque et sudores." Omnium sententiis absolutus itaque est. Profecto opera, non inpensa, cultura constat, et ideo maiores fertilissimum in agro oculum domini esse dixerunt.

4. TAKING GOOD CARE OF FARMING "TOOLS," ELDER PLINY, NATURAL HISTORY (NATURALIS HISTORIA) XVIII 41–43

I cannot refrain from bringing up one particular example from our ancestors; it will leave no doubt that in the past people were normally called to judge even about matters of agriculture. It also shows how those men of the past used to put up a defense. Caius Furius Cresimus, a former slave, reaped from his little field a much larger crop than his neighbors did from much bigger estates. So he was much disliked, as if he snatched other people's harvest by dark magic. For this reason, he was summoned to court by the aedile Spurius Albinus, and he feared he would be condemned by the vote of the tribes. He brought all the farming tools and his entire team of slaves into the forum. They were healthy, well tended, and well dressed, as Piso reports, with excellent iron tools, heavy plowshares, and strong oxen. Then he said: "this is my dark magic, citizens, and I cannot even show you by bringing into the forum the work I did in my sleepless nights and how much I sweated." He was unanimously acquitted. It is out of the question that agriculture depends on hard work, not on money, and for this reason our ancestors used to say that there is no better fertilizer in a field than the eye of the owner.

Text 5. Introduction: A Whisper from Voiceless Enslaved Laborers

The story of Furius Cresimus proves that a self-made man could be successful in ancient Rome. However, literary sources tend to pass over the quite different experience of the great majority of slaves working in the fields. For example, Cato lists different categories of people working on a farm, including the supervisor, the foreman, the shepherd, and the "chain gang." Cato gives very little information about these human beings, being primarily concerned with rationing their food; supervisors, foremen, and shepherds should be allotted three measures of bread per day, but chained slaves should receive four, surely on account of their harder labor. Cato spells out these numbers next to the amount of feed budgeted for cattle. Cato even specifies that slaves have to pay an owner to have sex with other slaves; in his logic, they should buy the right to enjoy the owner's property.

We have no account by a Roman slave regarding agricultural work, but comparative evidence helps us to make some informed guesses about their daily life. Frederick Douglass (ca. 1818–95), who was born a slave and wrote a memoir, narrates his different experiences depending on different masters. All masters worked Frederick very hard in the fields, but the better ones gave him enough food. "He, like Mr. Covey, gave us enough to eat; but, unlike Mr. Covey, he also gave us sufficient time to take our meals. . . . My treatment, while in his employment, was heavenly, compared with what I experienced at the hands of Mr. Edward Covey." The worse masters, however, starved their slaves: "Not to give a slave enough to eat, is regarded as the most aggravated development of meanness even among slaveholders."[8] Similarly, better masters refrained from physical abuse and tended to respect their slaves' family ties. Roman slaves, likewise left at the mercy of their owners, endured a comparable range of experiences with regard to nutrition, physical abuse, and chances to protect their families. Modern evidence, especially from Australia and from the southern United States, has cast some light on the subhuman conditions of chain gangs as well. People (especially convicts) toiled for long hours, while the shackles caused blisters and various infections, which could prove fatal.

Perhaps the condition of Roman slaves working in the fields improved over time. Writing about 250 years after Cato, Younger Pliny (selection 2) disregards chain gangs as old-fashioned; but chains remained legal, so that the treatment of slaves and laborers continued to depend on their master and on their supervisor, pretty much as in the narrative of Frederick Douglass. We have very few inscriptions from country slaves, but the epitaph reported below constitutes a rare piece of evidence and should be taken as an exception.

A WHISPER FROM THE ENSLAVED

HIPPOCRATI PLAVTI VILIC[VS] FAMILIA RVST[ICA]
QVIBVS IMPERAVIT MODESTE.

5. AN EPITAPH COMMEMORATING A GOOD SUPERVISOR, SELECTED LATIN INSCRIPTIONS (INSCRIPTIONES LATINAE SELECTAE) 7367

The rural slaves [dedicated this monument and inscription] to Hippocrates, the supervisor of Plautus. He ruled over them mildly.

Chapter 2

HOW TO BECOME RICH, PROBABLY ENVIED, AND PERHAPS RESPECTED

Commerce and Banking

Introduction

Sometime in the second century CE, a few Roman soldiers bought some commodities: towels, pepper, underwear, and beef fat cost 2 denarii each; an overcoat sold for 13 denarii, and a cloak for 5. Some of these items may have been produced locally, but pepper was imported and must have traveled all the way from India to Vindolanda, up in northern England, where the soldiers were stationed.

By the second century CE, commerce thrived. Olive oil, grain, wine, pottery, glass, and many other items regularly traveled within the borders of the Roman Empire, from Morocco to Armenia, from Iraq to Spain. Beyond its maintenance of a unified political control, the Empire promoted a common currency and common laws and regulations, which included low taxes on interprovincial trade. The central government also controlled piracy (at times successfully) and invested in an unprecedented network of roads, bridges, aqueducts, canals, and harbors. As a result, commerce thrived outside the borders of the Empire as well, and Roman coins have been found in Nigeria, Ghana, China, and Scandinavia. Above all, Romans exported wine and olive oil, but they imported pepper, ivory, and peacocks from India; cinnamon, frankincense, and myrrh from South Arabia; gold and ivory from southern Libya; and slaves from everywhere.

Whether or not all roads led to Rome, Rome unquestionably placed itself at the center of a transcontinental network. Over the centuries, the Romans built more than fifty thousand miles of roads and around one thousand bridges. To put these numbers into some perspective, the longest American interstate, I-90, stretches 3,022 miles and connects Boston and Seattle, and to date, the US interstate system as a whole is 46,876 miles long. An old truism holds that Roman roads were built for the army, so that soldiers could move quickly to critical areas. They were built for the army in another sense, as well, as paving new roads became a convenient means of keeping the soldiers occupied, lest the boys grow idle and idleness foster mutinies.

Military and financial considerations went hand in hand. This efficient highway network that connected all the provinces promoted commerce as well. For example, the ancient geographer Strabo writes that

Augustus refrained from invading England because he estimated that netting a 25 percent tax on international trade was more lucrative than annexing the territory, given that creating a new province implied investing in infrastructure and maintaining an army in situ.[9] On the other hand, Romans did not hesitate to construct water points and garrisons throughout the Egyptian desert and even provided armed escorts to safeguard the connection with Arabia and India. It has been calculated that the annual income on import and export taxes from this connection, known as the Red Sea route, amounted to roughly a quarter of the annual budget for the entire Roman army.

Commerce went along with banking as well. Merchants often bought cargo with loans taken from friends, middlemen, or professional bankers. Whoever the lender, special provisions existed for loans on sea cargo, known as "maritime loans." Maritime loan contracts spelled out the details of the transaction, including the origin and destination of a journey, the interest rates, the deadlines for payments, and late fees. In turn, laws regulated controversial cases and established common parameters, including maximum rates of interest. For example, the shipowner bore the entire risk of damage or loss of the ship. But if a cargo was lost for unforeseeable causes, such as a shipwreck or piracy, the loss fell on the investor. Since, as a rule, cargo was more valuable than ships, investors regularly sent commissioners on the journey; if an investor suspected that a merchant had been negligent (e.g., by overloading a ship) or fraudulent (e.g., by faking loss), they could sue. Typically, loans covered the expense for an outward cargo or a return cargo or both with the shipping costs. To obtain a loan, merchants pledged some property (typically the cargo or the ship). Upon reaching the destination and selling the goods, the merchant repaid the loan along with interest, accounted for any other incurred cost, and kept the rest as profit. In other words, commerce and finance supported each other, and both flourished.

Overseas trade carried a high risk for investors, and as one would expect, interest rates proportionately increased. Accordingly, Roman law allowed a unique rate for maritime loans. Instead of the usual 12 percent interest rate per year, maritime loans could have an interest rate of 25 percent. Another effect of the high risk (*periculum*) involved in overseas commerce is that both merchants and investors felt encouraged to join trade associations. By joining a consortium, merchants gained easier access to loans, distributed risks, and shared profits. Similarly, investors could lend out money on their own, or they could join a *societas*, a loan company formed of partners who pooled their resources and distributed the profit in proportion to their shares. A societas could afford to lend out more money than any of its shareholders individually, and everyone profited. Bankers financed not only trade, but also public constructions and military campaigns.

For that reason, individuals, societies, and the state itself relied on interest loans.

Clearly, moneylending was legal, lucrative and widespread. This fact may be hard to reconcile with the words of Cato (cited in the introduction) that compare moneylending to murder. It may be more surprising to discover that Cato himself used to lend out money "in the most shameful way, that is, on maritime loans."[10] It gets even worse: to reduce his risk, he forced merchants to join in companies and pledge ships as security; then he took a share in the company, not directly, but through Quintus, a former slave who acted as an agent and followed the merchants as a commissioner.

Was Cato a hypocrite? Did he change his mind over time? Or did he simply mean that a member of the Roman elite must own land and should never lend out money under his own name? Whatever one's verdict on Cato, his approach once again exemplifies a long-lasting Roman attitude. A Roman law originating in the Second Punic War banned senators from owning a cargo ship, commerce being deemed a less respectable pursuit. By the middle of the first century BCE the law had been disregarded, so in 59 BCE another law was passed to the same effect. Though the second law might have proven as ineffective, the stigma that gave rise to it persisted, as commerce continued to look less socially respectable than agriculture. Meanwhile, senators like Cato reaped spectacular profits by dodging legal restrictions and involving themselves in commerce and banking indirectly.

These senators, however, were only part of the picture since commerce and banking relied on a complex network of specialized workers. As selection 4 exemplifies, inscriptions and epitaphs commemorate the lives and labors of mule or horse drivers, litter bearers, animal tenders, and baggage handlers, along with different types of specialized wholesale and retail dealers, including those who traded food (e.g., meat, fish, olive oil, and wine), unguents and perfumes, books and papyrus, linens, silk and woolen goods, pigs and cattle, cosmetics and resins, and, finally, salt and salted fish. Similarly, bankers and joint stock companies employed various workers, such as treasurers, managers, guards, collectors, accountants, clerks, copyists, financial agents, and secretaries. These workers could be free or enslaved individuals, as shown in selection 6.

Text 1. Introduction: The Mobility, Pride, and Envy of a Self-Made Couple

Three vagabonds are the protagonists of Petronius's *Satyricon*, a Roman picaresque novel. In their wanderings, they happen to be invited to a dinner by a wealthy parvenu named Trimalchio. During the dinner they learn about his life and that of his wife, Fortunata. Their fictional stories parody personal narratives common in the Roman Empire, and the couple exemplifies the social mobility made possible by the risks and rewards of overseas trade. Perhaps Petronius, by caricaturing this self-made couple, suggests that people like Trimalchio and Fortunata can start from the very bottom of society and become rich through commerce, but that becoming part of the Roman elite is an altogether different matter.

Non potui amplius quicquam gustare, sed conversus ad eum, ut quam plurima exciperem, longe accersere fabulas coepi sciscitarique, quae esset mulier illa quae huc atque illuc discurreret. "Vxor, inquit, Trimalchionis, Fortunata appellatur, quae nummos modio metitur. Et modo, modo quid fuit? Ignoscet mihi genius tuus, noluisses de manu illius panem accipere. Nunc, nec quid nec quare, in caelum abiit et Trimalchionis topanta est. Ad summam, mero meridie si dixerit illi tenebras esse, credet. Ipse nescit quid habeat, adeo saplutus est; sed haec lupatria providet omnia, est ubi non putes. Est sicca, sobria, bonorum consiliorum: tantum auri vides. Est tamen malae linguae, pica pulvinaris. Quem amat, amat; quem non amat, non amat. Ipse Trimalchio fundos habet, quantum milvi volant, nummorum nummos. Argentum in ostiarii illius cella plus iacet, quam quisquam in fortunis habet. Familia vero—babae babae!—non mehercules puto decumam partem esse quae dominum suum noverit. Ad summam, quemvis ex istis babaecalis in rutae folium coniciet." ...

A SELF-MADE COUPLE

1. PORTRAYAL OF A SELF-MADE COUPLE, PETRONIUS, SATYRICON 37 AND 75–76

I was no longer able to enjoy any food. So I turned to another diner to draw as much info as possible out of him. I began to beat around the bush and asked: "Who's that woman, the one running here and there?" "She's the wife of Trimalchio; she's called Fortunata and counts her money by the bucket; but who was she, just a second ago? Please pardon me, but you would have refused to accept bread from her hand. And now, god knows how and why, she has been raised to the stars and is literally *everything* to Trimalchio. In short, if she told him that it's dark in the middle of the day, he'd believe her. And he's so loaded that he doesn't even know how much money he has. But this little bitch can take care of anything. You'll find her where you'd never expect. She's sober and clever and has a good head on her shoulders. What you see is pure gold, but she has a flapping tongue; she's the chatterbox of the party. Some people she happens to love, but others she just doesn't. Trimalchio's estates stretch as far as the eye can see. It's cash on top of cash; there's more silver in his porter's closet than anyone has in assets. And—my goodness!—he's got so many slaves! I'm afraid that not even one slave out of ten has ever met his master. In short, she can wrap any of those idiots here around her finger." . . .

"Sed ut coeperam dicere, ad hanc me fortunam frugalitas mea perduxit. Tam magnus ex Asia veni, quam hic candelabrus est. . . . Tamen ad delicias ipsimi annos quattuordecim fui. Nec turpe est, quod dominus iubet. Ego tamen et ipsimae satis faciebam. Scitis quid dicam: taceo, quia non sum de gloriosis. . . . Concupivi negotiari. Ne multis vos morer, quinque naves aedificavi, oneravi vinum — et tunc erat contra aurum — misi Romam. Putares me hoc iussisse: omnes naves naufragarunt. Factum, non fabula. Uno die Neptunus trecenties sestertium devoravit. Putatis me defecisse? Non mehercules mi haec iactura gusti fuit, tanquam nihil facti. Alteras feci maiores et meliores et feliciores, ut nemo non me virum fortem diceret. Scis, magna navis magnam fortitudinem habet. Oneravi rursus vinum, lardum, fabam, seplasium, mancipia. Hoc loco Fortunata rem piam fecit: omne enim aurum suum, omnia vestimenta vendidit et mi centum aureos in manu posuit. Hoc fuit peculii mei fermentum. Cito fit quod di volunt. Uno cursu centies sestertium corrotundavi. Statim redemi fundos omnes, qui patroni mei fuerant. Aedifico domum, venalicia coemo, iumenta; quicquid tangebam, crescebat tanquam favus."

Trimalchio: "But as I was just saying, what led me to this wealth is my worth. I arrived from Asia as rich as this candlestick. . . . When I was fourteen I became my master's sex slave, and there's nothing bad in complying with the will of a master. But I pleased the mistress as well. You know what I mean, so I say no more, because I'm not one who likes bragging. . . . I wanted to be a merchant. In short, I had five ships built, I loaded them with wine—which at the time was pure gold—and sent them to Rome. You would think that I planned this: they all sank. It's the truth; I'm not making things up. In one day Neptune gulped up thirty million. Do you think I gave up? By no means, and this loss left no more bitter taste in my mouth than if nothing had happened. I had other ships built, better and more promising so no one could say I'm no courageous man. As you know, a big ship has much capacity; I loaded it up with more wine, bacon, beans, unguents, and slaves. At this point Fortunata did a nice thing: she sold all her clothes and gold and put a hundred gold coins right in my hand. This was the yeast of my property. What the gods wish happens quickly: in one trip I made ten million. Right away, I bought back all the estates that used to belong to my master. I built myself a house, bought slaves and cattle. Whatever I touched grew just as a honeycomb."

Texts 2 and 3. Introduction:
Legal Writings on Maritime Loans

Romans had different ways of passing legislation, and laws had different names depending on the way they were enacted. During the Republic (traditionally 509–31 BCE), popular assemblies passed *leges*; the council of the plebs passed *plebiscita*; magistrates passed *edicta* and could ratify recommendations by the senate, *senatus consulta*. In practice there was little difference distinguishing the foregoing acts, because each had the force of a law. Theoretically, these means of passing legislation remained available during the Empire (traditionally 31 BCE–476 CE), but they became more and more obsolete, because emperors quickly became the sole source of law. Emperors passed laws by proclaiming edicts, by writing instructions to provincial governors (or other high state officials), by responding to legal inquiries, and by making decisions in their capacity as judge.

As one can imagine, by the beginning of the sixth century CE, the glorious corpus of Roman law was a tangly jungle of rules, poorly ordered and filled with redundancies and contradictions. For this reason, when Justinian became emperor of the Eastern Empire in 527, he appointed a commission to collect, edit, and organize this jungle. By Justinian's death (565 CE), lawyers and jurists had produced three bodies of legal writings, the *Codex*, the *Digesta*, and the *Institutes*.

Those Roman laws that were selected and polished by the commission were published thematically in twelve books, which make up the *Codex*. The *Digesta* ("abstracts"; singular *digestum*) collected fifty books of selections of legal writings by authoritative jurists who had discussed controversial issues. Finally, the three books of the *Institutes* were conceived as an introduction to the *Digesta* and written as a textbook for law students.

The next text (selection 2) comes from the *Codex*. Toward the end of the second century CE Diocletian and Maximianus gave a series of official responses to legal inquiries regarding maritime loans, and since they were emperors, these responses were laws. These laws were passed in different years and in reply to inquiries by different investors who wanted their money back. More than three hundred years later the jurists working for Justinian conveniently collected and grouped these responses under the title "about maritime loans," and in this form we still read them today. The first and second laws broke some bad news for the investors: a borrower had no obligation to repay a maritime loan until the boat and cargo safely reached their destination, and the risk of sailing is on the investor, not on the borrower. Hence, as seen above, investors sent commissioners and were ready to sue merchants if they failed to reach their destination owing to incompetence, negligence, or fraud. This is precisely the case in the third reported law, wherein the investor wins against the borrower. The last law specifies that borrowers enjoyed special protection for their cargo only if they signed a maritime loan. Remarkably, the emperors replied to legal inquiries by investors that were both male and female (as shown by the selection below). In either case, their word became law.

Selection 3 is taken from the *Digesta*. Hence, it does not reproduce the text of a law but an abstract from one of the influential Roman lawyers who discussed controversial issues. Typically abstracts, such as the one selected, present fictional cases. Each case is meant to draw out a problem and lay out a clear opinion by an authoritative jurist, such as Ulpian or Paul, whose opinions make up more than half of the *Digesta*. For example, book 22, from which selection 3 has been excerpted, deals with controversial cases regarding interests and loans, among other subjects.

Paul imagines a merchant who pledged a cargo for his ship. As mentioned, if a journey failed because of shipwreck or piracy, by law the investor bore the loss. But what if a merchant failed to purchase an adequate cargo and hence did not make enough money to pay off the loan (with maritime interests, of course)? To face this risk, the fictional investor demanded more security, and the fictional merchant pledged other cargos from other ships that had already been pledged to other lenders. This suggests that the borrower belonged to a merchant societas and hence was able to pledge cargos to be transported by his *socii*, or business partners, even if those had already been pledged to other investors. This also suggests that, regardless of the success of one's journey, socii shared the risks and the profits of their cumulative business. This arrangement lowered risks for a merchant, but what about the investor? By demanding more security and requesting an extra pledge on other cargos, the investor tried to gain access to the aggregate profits of the merchant's societas, to which he or she would otherwise have no claim. Imagine that the merchant duly purchased an adequate cargo to pay off the entire loan and was returning on time, but the ship was lost at sea. Who would bear the loss? The investor or the societas? The jurist Paul explains under which conditions an investor could have a claim on the profits of a borrower's societas.

A. Imperatores Diocletianus, Maximianus Scribonio Honorato

Traiecticiam pecuniam, quae periculo creditoris datur, tamdiu liberam esse ab observatione communium usurarum, quamdiu navis ad portum appulerit, manifestum est. * diocl. et maxim. aa. scribonio honorato. * <a 286 pp. iiii id. mart. maximo ii et aquilino conss.>

B. Imperatores Diocletianus, Maximianus

Cum dicas pecuniam te ea lege dedisse, ut in sacra urbe tibi restitueretur, nec incertum periculum, quod ex navigatione maris metui solet, ad te pertinuisse profitearis, non dubium est pecuniae creditae ultra licitum te usuras exigere non posse. * diocl. et maxim. aa. aureliae cosmianae. * <a 286 pp. prid. id. mart. maximo ii et aquilino conss.>

C. Imperatores Diocletianus, Maximianus

Cum proponas te nauticum fenus ea condicione dedisse, ut post navigium, quod in africam dirigi debitor adseverabat, in salonitanorum portum nave delata fenebris pecunia tibi redderetur, ita ut navigii dumtaxat quod in africam destinabatur periculum susceperis, perque vitium debitoris, nec loco quidem

2. IMPERIAL LAWS ON MARITIME LOANS LENT OUT BY MALE OR FEMALE INVESTORS, JUSTINIAN CODE (CODEX JUSTINIANI) IV 33

A. Emperors Diocletian and Maximian to Scribonius Honoratus

Maritime loans, which are granted at the risk of investors, are clearly not bound to ordinary loan regulations, until a ship enters the harbor. May 11, 286, when Maximus and Aquilinus were consuls.

B. Emperors Diocletian and Maximian [to Aurelia Cosmiana]

Since you say that you lent out money on condition that it be returned to you in Rome and since you declare that you were not unaware of the risks that people fear in sea journeys, there is no doubt that, for the money you lent, you are not allowed to demand interest beyond what is established by law. Emperors Diocletian and Maximian responded to Aurelia Cosmiana on March 14, 286, when Maximus and Aquilinus were consuls.

C. Emperors Diocletian and Maximian [to Aurelia Juliana]

You report that you granted a maritime loan on condition that, after the journey to Africa, according to the borrower's stated plan, the money plus the interest would be returned to you when the ship entered the port of Salona [in Croatia]. You undertook the risk

navigii servato, illicitis comparatis mercibus quae navis continebat fiscum occupasse: amissarum mercium detrimentum, quod non ex marinae tempestatis discrimine, sed ex praecipiti avaritia et incivili debitoris audacia accidisse adseveratur, adscribi tibi iuris publici ratio non permittit. * diocl. et maxim. aa. aureliae iulianae. *

D. Imperatores Diocletianus, Maximianus

Traiecticiae quidem pecuniae, quae periculo creditoris mutuo datur, casus, antequam, ad destinatum locum navis perveniat, ad debitorem non pertinet, sine huiusmodi vero conventione infortunio naufragii non liberabitur. * diocl. et maxim. aa. et cc. pullio iuliano eucharisto. * <a 294 d. viii id. oct. retiariae cc. conss.>

Faenerator pecuniam usuris maritimis mutuam dando quasdam merces in nave pignori accepit, ex quibus si non potuisset totum debitum exsolvi, aliarum mercium aliis navibus impositarum propriisque faeneratoribus obligatarum si quid superfuisset, pignori

of the journey to the extent that it was directed to Africa. You also report that, because of the fault of the borrower, who did not even have regard for the agreed destination and acquired some unlawful goods, the state confiscated the cargo carried by the ship. Hence, the loss of the cargo was not caused by the hazard of a tempest but by the borrower's inconsiderate greed and fraudulent daring; therefore, by law, this loss cannot fall on you. Emperors Diocletian and Maximian responded to Aurelia Juliana. [Date not specified.]

D. Emperors Diocletian and Maximian [to Pullius Julianus Eucharistus]

A loss of a maritime loan, which is lent at the investor's risk, does not fall on the borrower until a ship reaches its destination, but without a maritime contract, a borrower will not be secured against the misfortune of a shipwreck. Emperors Diocletian and Maximian responded to Pullius Julianus Eucharistus on October 8, 294.

3. A LEGAL OPINION ON THE PAYMENT OF MARITIME LOANS, DIGEST OF ROMAN LAWS (DIGESTA) XXII 2.6

An investor lent money at a maritime rate and took a portion of the cargo as a deposit; also, in case the entire debit could not be paid by this cargo, he took as a collateral other merchandise from other ships. If this merchandise, which had been pledged to other

accepit. Quaesitum est nave propria perempta, ex qua totum solvi potuit, an id damnum ad creditorem pertineat, intra praestitutos dies amissa nave, an ad ceterarum navium superfluum admitti possit. Respondi: alias quidem pignoris deminutio ad damnum debitoris, non etiam ad creditoris pertinet: sed cum traiecticia pecunia ita datur, ut non alias petitio eius creditori competat, quam si salva navis intra statuta tempora pervenerit, ipsius crediti obligatio non exsistente condicione defecisse videtur, et ideo pignorum quoque persecutio perempta est etiam eorum, quae non sunt amissa. Si navis intra praestitutos dies perisset, et condicionem stipulationis defecisse videri, ideoque sine causa de pignorum persecutione, quae in aliis navibus fuerunt, quaeri. Quando ergo ad illorum pignorum persecutionem creditor admitti potuerit? Scilicet tunc cum condicio exstiterit obligationis et alio casu pignus amissum fuerit vel vilius distractum vel si navis postea perierit, quam dies praefinitus periculo exactus fuerit.

lenders, reached its destination safely, what remained after paying the other lenders was pledged to the investor. Imagine that the first ship, from which the entire debt could be paid, was lost within the contracted deadline. The question is whether this loss falls on the investor or whether it can be credited to the cargo that survived on other ships. My reply: aside from *cause majeure* cases [e.g., shipwreck or pirates], loss of a collateral certainly falls on the debtor, not on the investor. But since a maritime loan is granted on the condition that an investor's request for the collateral is not binding unless the ship has arrived safely and by a set deadline, it is clear that the contract of this loan is void, since it did not meet one of the terms, and as a consequence, the seizure of the other collateral for merchandise that was not lost is equally void. In the same way, if the ship was lost before the deadline, but the terms of the contract were not met, there is no ground to claim the deposit from the other ships' cargos. In which case, then, can a lender lay claim for security from those other cargos? Clearly, when a stipulation from a contract stands and the pledged merchandise gets lost by other occurrence or is retailed too cheaply or if the ship is ruined after the established deadline.

Text 4. Introduction: The Epitaph of Megiste, a Greengrocer

Upon reaching its destination, a cargo would be sold to retail dealers, such as Megiste, who specialized in grain and pulse. In commemorating Megiste, Marcus Abudius styles himself her "patron and husband." Ancient Roman law did not recognize slaves' marriages, and Marcus's language makes it clear that he used to own Megiste as a slave, but he freed and married her legally—which was not uncommon. Marcus has no filiation in his name, which suggests that perhaps he used to be a slave as well (or a descendant of a freedman). However, Marcus and Megiste's son was enrolled in the elder body of the Esquiline tribe, hence he was born free and even belonged to a privileged group (the honor of "seniority" did not necessarily depend on age). This epitaph, which is longer than many others, and the references to the family tomb and to the freed slaves come together to demonstrate that Megiste and Marcus did well. Megiste ran a successful business, and Marcus specifies its location "at the middle stair," but this location has not been surely identified.

THE EPITAPH OF MEGISTE

DIS MANIBVS
ABVDIAE M(ARCI) LIB(ERTAE)
MEGISTE PIISSIMAE FEC(IT)
M(ARCVS) ABVDIVS LVMINARIS
PATRONVS IDEMQVE
CONIVX BENE MERENTI
NEGOTIATRICI FRVMENTARIAE
ET LEGVMENARIA[E] AB SCALA
MEDIANA SIBI ET LIBERTIS
LIBERTABVSQVE POSTERISQ(VE)
ET M(ARCO) ABVDIO SATVRNINO
FILIO TRIB(V) ESQ(VILINA) SENIORVM
VIXIT ANNIS VIII

4. A BUSINESSWOMAN, MOVING FROM SLAVERY TO SUCCESS, CORPUS OF LATIN INSCRIPTIONS (CORPUS INSCRIPTIONUM LATINARUM) VI.2.9683

TO THE DIVINE SPIRITS
OF ABUDIA MEGISTE, MOST DUTIFUL
FREEDWOMAN OF MARCUS,
MARCUS ABUDIUS LUMINARIS, HER PATRON
AND LIKEWISE HUSBAND
MADE (THIS MONUMENT) FOR HER
A WELL-DESERVING
DEALER IN GRAIN
AND PULSES AT THE MIDDLE STAIR
FOR HIMSELF
AND HIS FREEDMEN
AND FREEDWOMEN AND DESCENDANTS
AND FOR MARCUS ABUDIUS SATURNINUS
HIS SON, FELLOW TRIBESMAN OF THE ESQUILINE
  TRIBE, OF THE BODY OF ELDERS,
WHO LIVED EIGHT YEARS

Texts 5 and 6. Introduction: Public Contracts and Joint Stock Companies

By extending its supremacy over the Mediterranean, Rome brought in money from war booty but had to invest first in military operations and then in infrastructure. As a result, the business of state contracting boomed both within and outside of Italy. For example, in 105 BCE, two local magistrates from Puteoli (a small town on the Bay of Naples) commissioned the construction of a wall to a company of contractors. A council formed by twenty local senators approved the contract, which is reported in selection 5. Contractors relied on professional staff, including scribes, secretaries, accountants, and various builders. The last selection (6) is an epitaph dedicated to a certain Cestus, a slave secretary, by a slave comrade. The short inscription does not mention which type of secretary Cestus was, but it specifies that he died when he was twenty-two (in his twenty-third year, by Roman counting) and that he was a good friend.

As typical, the contract begins with a date, which grafts the local calendar onto central Roman time; it was issued ninety years after the foundation of Puteoli (i.e., in 105 BCE, as Puteoli was founded in 194), when Fufidius and Pollius were town magistrates and Rutilius and Manlius were Roman consuls. Next, the magistrates give a detailed description of the job to be completed, specifying the wall's position, measurements, and materials, and setting out the conditions of the contract; they establish the *dies operis*, or completion deadline, and the *dies pecuniae*, or payment date, upon satisfaction of *probatio*, or official inspection. The inspection was usually conducted by the magistrates who signed the contract or by their successors, but magistrates could equally appoint a committee of experts who assessed the quality of the work.

Contractors knew that they had to take probatio very seriously; approval depended entirely on the satisfaction of the *probatores*, and there is no evidence of any mechanism for appeals. The agreed sum was to be disbursed in two payments. Contractors would receive the first half upon signing the contract and the second after successful probatio. Since contractors received public money before completing a work, they entered their bid for contract only after making a pledge, *praedium* (plural *praedia*), consisting of land given as security. The document ends with the names of five contractors and specifies the shares each had in the company. Mind the small print: probatores are on their way.

AB COLONIA DEDVCTA ANNO XC, / N. FVFIDIO N. F.,
M. POLLIO DVOVIR[EIS], / P. RVTILIO, CN. MALLIO
CO[N]S[VLIBVS]. / OPERVM LEX 112.

LEX PARIETI FACIENDO IN AREA QVAE EST ANTE /
AEDEM SERAPI TRANS VIAM. QVI REDEMERIT, / PRAEDES
DATO PRAEDIAQVE SVBSIGNATO / DVVMVIRVM ARBI-
TRATV. /

IN AREA TRANS VIAM PARIES QVI EST PROPTER /
VIAM, IN EO PARIETE MEDIO OSTIEI LVMEN / APERITO;
LATVM P[EDES] VI, ALTVM P[EDES] VII FACITO. EX EO
/ PARIETE ANTAS DVAS AD MARE VORSVM PROICITO /
LONGAS P[EDES] II, CRASSAS P[EDEM] I [QVADRANTEM].

INSVPER ID LIMEN / ROBVSTVM LONG[VM] P[EDES]
VIII, LATVM P[EDEM] I [QVADRANTEM], ALTVM P[EDIS]
[DODRANTEM] IMPONITO.

INSVPER ID ET ANTAS MVTVLOS ROBVSTOS / II,
CRASSOS [BESSEM], ALTOS P[EDEM] I PROICITO EXTRA
PARIETE / IN VTRAMQ[VE] PARTEM P[EDES] IV.

INSVPER SIMAS PICTAS / FERRO OFFIGITO. INSVPER
MVTVLOS TRABICVLAS / ABIEGINEAS II, CRASSAS QVOQVE
VERSVS S[EMISSEM], INPONITO // FERROQVE FIGITO.

5. AN INSCRIPTION WITH A CONTRACT BETWEEN A TOWN AND A JOINT STOCK COMPANY, INSCRIPTIONS OF THE ROMAN REPUBLIC (INSCRIPTIONES LATINAE LIBERAE REI PUBLICAE) 518 = CORPUS OF LATIN INSCRIPTIONS (CORPUS INSCRIPTIONUM LATINARUM) I.698.1.12

Year 90 since the foundation of the colony, when Numerius Fufidius, son of Numerius, and Marcus Pollius were town magistrates and when Publius Rutilius and Cneus Manlius were consuls [105 BCE]. Procurement contract number 2.

Contract for the construction of a wall in the area across the street in front of the temple of Serapis. The two above-mentioned magistrates will decide how much money and land are pledged as guarantee by the contractors for undertaking this construction.

Create an opening in the middle of the wall that is found just across the street. Measures: six feet wide and seven feet high. To this wall, attach two columns stretching out in the direction of the sea; the columns will be two feet long and a quarter of a foot thick.

Over this opening, place a doorway base in oak wood, eight feet long, a quarter of a foot wide, and three-fourths of a foot high.

Over this base build in square pilasters, and place two modillions in oak wood: each modillion will be two-thirds of a foot thick, one foot high, and stretching out from the wall for four feet in each direction.

Inasserato asseribvs abiegniteis / sectilibvs, crasseis qvoqve versvs [trientem]; disponito ni plvs [dodrantem]. / Opercvlaqve abiegnea inponito. Ex tigno pedario / facito.

Antepagmenta abiegnea lata [dodrantem], crassa [semvnciam] / cvmativmqve inponito ferroqve plano figito, / portvla[m]qve tegito tegvlarvm ordinibvs seneis / qvoqve versvs. Tegvlas primores omnes in ante/pagmento ferro figito marginemqve inponito. Eisdem fores clatatras ii cvm postibvs aescvlnieis / facito, statvito, oclvdito picatoqve ita, vtei ad aedem / Honorvs facta svnt. Eisdem maceria extrema paries / qvi est, evm parietem cvm margine altvm facito p[edes] X. / Eisdem ostivm, introitv in area qvod nvnc est, et / fenestras, qvae in pariete propter eam aream svnt, / pariete[m] opstrvito; et parieti, qvi nvnc est propter / viam, marginem perpetvom inponito.

Eosq[ve] parietes / marginesqve omnes, qvae lita non ervnt, calce / harenato lita politaqve at calce vda dealbata recte / facito. Qvod opvs strvctile fiet, in ter[r]a calcis, / restinctai partem qvartam indito. Nive maiorem / caementa[m] strvito, qvam qvae cementa arda / pendat p[ondo] xv, nive angolaria[m] altiorem [trientem seminciam] facito. // Locvmqve pvrvm pro eo opere reddito. / Eidem sacella, aras signaqve, qvae in / campo sunt, qvae demonstrata ervnt, / ea

Fasten painted moldings above with iron nails, place above the modillions two cylindrical beams of silver fir with a half-foot diameter, and fasten them with iron nails as well. Cover with cylindrical silver fir beams, which have been cut into thin layers and with a diameter of a third of a foot. Arrange those with intervals of no more than nine inches. Fasten a cover of silver fir above using a one-foot-long timber.

Place the molding and the overhanging ornaments in silver fir, nine inches wide and six inches thick, fasten them entirely with iron nails, and cover the small entrance with rows of six roof tiles in either direction. Fasten the first row of roof tiles with iron nail into the ornaments, and place the edge on top. Build two doors for them with railings and with door posts in winter oak wood; set this up, secure it, and spread a layer of pitch to make it waterproof, just as they did with the temple of Honor. As for the top of the brick wall, build it ten feet high and with an edge. Build a wall against the area that is now an entrance and against the windows that are nearby in the wall. Fasten an uninterrupted edge to the wall by the street.

Plaster all these walls and edges, which will not be coated, smear them with lime mixed with sand, make it smooth and polished, and carefully prime it with wet white lime. For making cement, add a fourth part of slaked lime into soil. Do not apply more cement than fifteen pounds before you add any water, and place no more than four and a half inches on the corners.

OMNIA TOLLITO, DEFERTO, COMPONITO / STATVITO-
QVE, VBEI LOCVS DEMONSTRATVS ERIT, DVVMVIRVM
ARBITRATV. /

HOC OPVS OMNE FACITO ARBITRATV DVOVIR[VM] /
ET DVOVIRA[L]IVM, QVI IN CONSILIO ESSE / SOLENT
PVTEOLEIS, DVM NI MINVS VIGINTI / ADSIENT, CUM
EA RES CONSVLETVR. QVOD / EORVM VIGINTI IVRATI
PROBAVERINT, PROBVM / ESTO; QVOD IEIS INPROBAR-
INT, INPROBVM ESTO. / DIES OPERIS: K[ALENDIS]
NOVEMBR[IBVS] PRIMEIS. DIES PECVN[IAE]: PARS
DIMIDIA DABITVR, VBEI PRAEDIA SATIS / SVBSIGNATA
ERVNT; ALTERA PARS DIMIDIA SOLVETVR / OPERA EF-
FECTO PROBATOQVE.

C. BLOSSIVS Q. F. / [SESTERTIIS] MD, IDEM PRAES,
Q. FVFICIVS Q. F. / CN. TETTEIVS Q. F., C. GRANIVS
C. F., TI. CRASSICIVS.

Leave the area in front of this work clean. Chapels, altars, and statues that are in this location and which will be indicated need to be removed, carried away, reassembled, and stationed in a place to be chosen and shown by the two town magistrates.

Complete this work according to the will of the two town magistrates and of the individuals on their staff who normally sit in the council of the town of Puteoli. There must be a quorum of twenty to consider the matter. What twenty of those individuals officially approve will be properly built; what does not satisfy their standard will not. Deadline for completion: first of November. Dates of payment: half will be disbursed when the contract for pledging land is signed, and the second half once the work has been completed and approved.

Caius Blossius, son of Quintus, has a share of 1,500 sestertii; the same share have Quintus Fuficius, son of Quintus; Cneus Tetteius, son of Quintus; Caius Granius, son of Caius; and Titus Crassicius.

PUBLIC CONTRACTS

Cesto L(vci) Volvsi
Satvrnini servo
a manv
annor(vm) xxiii
Tryphaena cons(ervo)
d(e) s(e) b(ene) m(erenti)

6. A FEMALE SLAVE COMMEMORATES A FELLOW (MALE) SLAVE, WHO WORKED AS A SECRETARY, CORPUS OF LATIN INSCRIPTIONS (CORPUS INSCRIPTIONUM LATINARUM) VI.14711

(DEDICATED) TO CESTUS
SLAVE SECRETARY OF
LUCIUS VOLUSIUS
SATURNINUS
HE WAS TWENTY-TWO YEARS OLD
TRYPHAENA (BUILT THIS) WITH HER OWN MONEY
    FOR HER FELLOW SLAVE
WHO WELL DESERVED IT FROM HER

Chapter 3

HOW TO BECOME RICH, MAYBE ENVIED, BUT CERTAINLY NOT RESPECTED

Taxation and Public Contracts

Introduction

Romans imposed two main types of taxes, *tributa* (singular *tributum*) and *vectigalia* (singular *vectigal*). Tributum was either a land tax (*tributum soli*) or a poll tax (*tributum capitis*). A vectigal was collected for special services ensured by the state. For example, farmers paid reasonable vectigalia for letting their cattle graze on public land or for renting a plot belonging to the state; masters paid a tax on manumitted slaves (*vicesima libertatis*); and merchants paid *portoria*, or import-export tax, which amounted to around 2.5 percent for interprovincial trade and up to 25 percent on international trade.

After being collected locally, tributa and vectigalia were both stored in a common treasury, called the *aerarium*. Under the Republic (509–31 BCE), two officials, called urban questors, managed the budget revenue, and the senate controlled the expenditures. In particular, the senate was responsible for deciding how much to allot to consuls on military campaigns and to censors for contracting out construction and repair work on public buildings. Under the reign of Augustus (31 BCE–14 CE), however, the senate lost effective control of finances, and Roman emperors took charge of the aerarium.

In practice, the revenue system was rather complicated, because the central government struck special treaties with individuals, towns, colonies, and provinces, and these treaties ranged from very favorable to very unfavorable. For instance, a town could be allowed to collect and keep the vectigalia on trade, but a nearby town might not enjoy the same privilege. There could be different reasons for these different treatments. For example, the two towns may have provided unequal support to Roman troops centuries before. As a result, the fiscal map of the Roman Empire resembled a quilt of statutes spelling out specific and expandable taxes and exemptions. This meant that certain communities would nourish hopes and concerns regarding their relation with Rome, but that these hopes and concerns might not be the same as those of their neighbors. However, one thing that all these communities shared was the knowledge that Roman rulers rewarded loyalty and punished resistance.

Perhaps no other practice embodies the famous Roman proverb *divide et impera*, or "divide and rule," better than this policy of fiscal fragmentation. By disseminating local disunity and fostering loyalty to the center, the Romans turned taxation into an effective instrument of imperial sovereignty.

The method of tax collecting further complicated the picture. Romans began to annex provinces before they had developed an imperial fiscal system. Hence, they found it convenient to employ private companies of tax farmers, or *publicani*. Companies of publicani competed for the job, and the highest bidder bought a public contract for collecting revenue. They were theoretically supposed to collect 10 percent, which was the maximum tax rate fixed by a censorial law; in practice, however, they often asked for more, because whatever revenue exceeded the contract counted as profit, and all the profit was distributed among the members of a company.

Texts 1 and 2. Introduction: The Power of the Publicani

Publicani were renowned for being powerful, but they were hated and perceived as greedy and dishonest. Cicero, who was a senator, treated them with diplomatic deference; but to appreciate the point of view of provincial taxpayers we can turn to the Gospels, where publicani are regularly lumped together with sinners and prostitutes.

Around 60 BCE, Cicero wrote a letter (selection 1) to his brother Quintus, who had recently been appointed governor of Asia (broadly corresponding to modern-day Turkey). Cicero's letter reads like a miniature treatise on good government, and part of his lecture concerns the thorny problem of tax revenues. Governors, like his brother Quintus, had to rely on publicani, while provincials, often overwhelmed by their abuses, regularly complained to the governor. Cicero diplomatically recommended that his brother employ his "quasi-divine wisdom"; yet Cicero was perhaps more concerned about his own relationship with the publicani than about the well-being of the provincials. Accordingly, he volunteered his suggestions for some arguments and phrasing to persuade the provincials to comply with the system and just reconcile themselves to paying taxes. Moreover, Cicero took the side of the publicani when it came to the most controversial issue—what if the publicani attempted to collect more than what had been established by law? Would a governor stand up to them and support the people, or would he turn a blind eye to their mischiefs and let the provincials down?

Because of the wealth, political connections, and strong corporate organization of the publicani, it was difficult for even a governor to confront them. Roman governors were appointed to oversee a province for a few years (typically one to three), while publicani enjoyed a stable presence, great resources, and a solid network. For these reasons, they dominated finance in the provinces. Publicani even lent out money to allied kings and states (as will be shown in selection 2). Traditionally, publicani belonged to the *ordo equestris*, or equestrian order (the Roman "class of knights"), but many senators were (more or less directly) involved in their companies. Thus, the two most influential Roman classes were invested in the success of the publicani.

An efficient corporate organization further increased the power of the publicani. A *manceps*, or official bidder, acted on behalf of the shareholders, socii, who elected one or more *magistri*, or masters, to govern the societas. Larger companies had various offices, each run by a *pro magistro*, or local master, who managed the staff. The staff could comprise hundreds of employees, including freeborn persons, freedmen, and slaves, working as managers, accountants, door-to-door collectors, or messengers. Messengers, *tabellarii*, were particularly important for ensuring communication and transportation of goods, cash, contracts, and accounts, which were recorded on small boards called *tabellae*. Indeed, the postal system developed by the publicani was so efficient that in the Republic their tabellarii also regularly carried mail for government officials. One can begin to see why Cicero recommended that his brother adopt a diplomatic approach.

Moreover, since the state was responsible for political order, if tax collection was hindered by war or rebellion, the state bore the loss and returned the investment to the publicani. And if a foreign king borrowed from a societas but was then unable to solve a debt, would the publicani enjoy Roman protection? This is precisely what happened with Ptolemy XII, the king of Egypt. Having been expelled by his people in 58 BCE, Ptolemy traveled to Rome, borrowed heavily from a societas of publicani, and generously bribed Roman politicians who could restore him to power. Rabirius Postumus was a prominent member of the lending societas, but he overinvested in Ptolemy and struggled to regain both his own money and that of his socii (selection 2). So he went to Egypt, but Ptolemy did not pay the loan. Instead, he allowed Postumus to collect taxes from Egyptians, and Postumus took his chances. The people of Alexandria were so overwhelmed at his exactions that they rebelled. Pressed by popular anger, Ptolemy arrested Postumus, but he secretly let him flee to Rome. The Roman senate was embarrassed and prosecuted Postumus for corruption and extortion. But Postumus belonged to the influential equestrian order and found the best lawyer in town, Cicero. To defend his client (54 BCE), Cicero appealed to the sympathy of the equestrians serving in the jury. Postumus was acquitted.

Atque huic tuae voluntati ac diligentiae difficultatem magnam adferunt publicani. Quibus si adversamur, ordinem de nobis optime meritum et per nos cum re publica coniunctum et a nobis et a re publica diiungemus; sin autem omnibus in rebus obsequemur, funditus eos perire patiemur quorum non modo saluti sed etiam commodis consulere debemus. Haec est una, si vere cogitare volumus, in toto imperio tuo difficultas. Nam esse abstinentem, continere omnis cupiditates, suos coercere, iuris aequabilem tenere rationem, diligentem te in rebus cognoscendis, <facilem> in hominibus audiendis admittendisque praebere praeclarum magis est quam difficile. Non est enim positum in labore aliquo sed in quadam inductione animi et voluntate. Illa causa publicanorum quantam acerbitatem adferat sociis intelleximus ex civibus qui nuper in portoriis Italiae tollendis non tam de portorio quam de non nullis iniuriis portitorum querebantur. Qua re non ignoro quid sociis accidat in ultimis terris, cum audierim in Italia querelas civium. Hic te ita versari ut et publicanis satis facias, praesertim publicis male redemptis, et socios perire non sinas divinae cuiusdam virtutis esse videtur, id est tuae.

Ac primum Graecis id quod acerbissimum est, quod sunt vectigales, non ita acerbum videri debet,

THE POWER OF THE PUBLICANI

1. HOW TO DEAL WITH TAX COLLECTORS, CICERO, LETTERS TO HIS BROTHER QUINTUS (EPISTULAE AD QUINTUM FRATREM) I 1.32–35

But the publicans present a serious threat to your goodwill and care. If we resist them, we alienate from us and from the state a class that has wonderfully supported us and which, with my mediation, has been allied with the state. Completely complying with them, however, amounts to throwing to the wolves the very people we are supposed to protect and favor. To be honest, this is the most serious challenge in your office. Indeed, remaining uncorrupted and reining in greed, controlling your staff and being a fair judge, carefully assessing each situation and remaining available to the people—all this is truly honorable, but not really difficult, because it does not depend on hard work, but on personal disposition and will. But a certain episode taught us how much resentment publicans can generate in provincials. Citizens recently complained about import taxes in Italy; they were not upset by the taxes per se, but by the abuses of the collectors. Having heard complaints of this sort in Italy, I can imagine how our allies are treated in faraway provinces. In this matter, to succeed in letting the publicans get their money, especially when a state contract was not drafted lawfully, and to prevent the ruin of the taxpayers requires quasi-divine wisdom, just like yours.

propterea quod sine imperio populi Romani suis institutis per se ipsi ita fuerunt. Nomen autem publicani
aspernari non possunt, qui pendere ipsi vectigal sine
publicano non potuerint quod iis aequaliter Sulla
discripserat. Non esse autem leniores in exigendis
vectigalibus Graecos quam nostros publicanos hinc
intellegi potest quod Caunii nuper omnibusque ex
insulis quae erant a Sulla Rhodiis attributae confugerunt
ad senatum, nobis ut potius vectigal quam Rhodiis
penderent. Qua re nomen publicani neque ii debent
horrere qui semper vectigales fuerunt, neque ii aspernari qui per se pendere vectigal non potuerunt, neque
ii recusare qui postulaverunt.

Simul et illud Asia cogitet, nullam ab se neque belli
externi neque domesticarum discordiarum calamita-
tem afuturam fuisse, si hoc imperio non teneretur; id
autem imperium cum retineri sine vectigalibus nullo
modo possit, aequo animo parte aliqua suorum fruc-
tuum pacem sibi sempiternam redimat atque otium.
Quod si genus ipsum et nomen publicani non iniquo
animo sustinebunt, poterunt iis consilio et prudentia
tua reliqua videri mitiora. Possunt in pactionibus fa-
ciendis non legem spectare censoriam sed potius
commoditatem conficiendi negoti et liberationem mo-
lestiae. Potes etiam tu id facere, quod et fecisti egregie
et facis, ut commemores quanta sit in publicanis dig-
nitas, quantum nos illi ordini debeamus, ut remoto
imperio ac vi potestatis et fascium publicanos cum
Graecis gratia atque auctoritate coniungas [sed] et ab

First off, the Greeks should learn that paying taxes, which they deem most repulsive, is not so bad, for the simple reason that, if the Roman Empire did not exist and they lived under their own institutions, they would still have to do so. They cannot disdain the very name "publican," given that when Sulla granted them the right to collect taxes directly without tax farmers, they did not manage. But in truth, what just happened leaves no doubt that the Greeks themselves are no more moderate in collecting taxes than our publicans are; the Cauni came from all the islands that had been put under the Rhodians and flooded the senate, begging that they pay taxes to us, rather than to the Rhodians. Therefore, those who have always been taxpayers should not dread the word "publican," and those who were unable to pay taxes according to their own system should not feel contempt toward tax collectors. They got what they asked for.

Equally, Asia should realize that, without being part of our empire, she would not escape foreign wars and internal conflicts. Since an empire can in no way be sustained without taxes, let Asia repay everlasting peace and security with a portion of its produce without quarreling. If they accept the system and the name of publicans without hostility, thanks to your wise diplomacy, everything else will seem more agreeable to them. In drafting the contracts for collecting taxes, they do not need to abide by the censorial law, but they can look for a way to accomplish the task

iis de quibus optime tu meritus es et qui tibi omnia debent hoc petas, ut facilitate sua nos eam necessitudinem quae est nobis cum publicanis obtinere et conservare patiantur.

Fuit enim pueris nobis huius pater, C. Curtius, princeps ordinis equestris, fortissimus et maximus publicanus, cuius in negotiis gerendis magnitudinem animi non tam homines probassent, nisi in eodem benignitas incredibilis fuisset, ut in augenda re non avaritiae praedam, sed instrumentum bonitati quaerere videretur. Hoc ille natus, quamquam patrem suum numquam viderat, tamen et natura ipsa duce, quae plurimum valet, et adsiduis domesticorum sermonibus in paternae disciplinae similitudinem deductus est. Multa gessit, multa contraxit, magnas partis habuit publicorum; credidit populis; in pluribus provinciis eius versata res est; dedit se etiam regibus; huic ipsi Alexandrino grandem iam antea pecuniam credidit; nec interea locupletare amicos umquam suos destitit, mittere in

conveniently and smoothly. You can also remind them of how highly respected the publicans are and how much our family owes them; you have been and continue to be outstanding at that. In this way, without dwelling on your office and the power that comes with it, you can reconcile Greeks and publicans relying on the influence of your authority. Also, you can request of the provincials, whom you have so favored and who are totally in your debt, that, by behaving graciously, they let us maintain our strong connection with the publicans.

2. *CICERO,* SPEECH IN DEFENSE OF RABIRIUS POSTUMUS *(PRO RABIRIO POSTUMO) 3–5*

When I was young, C. Curtius, the father of my client, was a leader of the equestrian class, a most eminent and worthy tax collector, and people would not have approved of his magnanimity in conducting business so much had he not also displayed incredible generosity. It was clear that in growing his wealth he did not strive to satisfy his greed but pursued the means to be generous. This is the man who gave birth to my client, and even if he never met his father, he was raised to imitate his paternal discipline. He followed his blood tie, which accounts for so very much, along with all he heard about his father in the household. My client has achieved a great deal: he won many bids for contracts; he held significant shares in companies of tax collectors; he financed peoples, so his patrimony

negotium, dare partis, augere <re>, fide sustentare. Quid multa? Cum magnitudine animi, tum liberalitate vitam patris et consuetudinem expresserat. Pulsus interea regno Ptolomaeus dolosis consiliis, ut dixit Sibylla, sensit Postumus, Romam venit. Cui egenti et roganti hic infelix pecuniam credidit, nec tum primum; nam regnanti crediderat absens; nec temere se credere putabat, quod erat nemini dubium quin is in regnum restitueretur a senatu populoque Romano. In dando autem et credendo processit longius nec suam solum pecuniam credidit sed etiam amicorum, stulte; quis negat, aut quis iam audebit, quod male cecidit, bene consultum putare? Sed est difficile, quod cum spe magna sis ingressu, id non exsequi usque ad extremum.

was poured into multiple provinces; he even financed kings, and in the past King Ptolemy of Alexandria borrowed much money from him. Meanwhile, he never stopped enriching his friends. He included them in his business, increasing their shares, distributing his, and vouching for them. Do I need to say more? Both in magnanimity and in generosity he imitated his father's life and approach. In the middle of all this, King Ptolemy was exiled from his own kingdom with a plan that the Sibylla defined as "wicked." Postumus came to know this, and Ptolemy traveled to Rome. My poor client lent money to Ptolemy when he was stretching out his hands in need, and it was not the first time, because he already lent to Ptolemy when Ptolemy was still ruling and without even meeting him in person. Postumus had reason to believe that this was not a bad investment, since no one doubted that the senate and the Roman people would restore Ptolemy in his kingdom. Still, in advancing and lending he went out of his way, and lent not only his own money, but also that of friends, and that was a mistake. Who denies it? And in hindsight who will have the courage to think that what turned out so poorly was actually well planned? But once one gets into something with great expectations, it is hard not to pursue it to the end.

Texts 3 and 4. Introduction:
Other Methods for Collecting Taxes

As has been seen, provincial governors regularly employed companies of publicani for lack of a better option, but nothing prohibited these governors from collecting revenue directly. This is precisely what one senator, Gaius Verres (ca. 119–43 BCE), attempted to do as governor of Sicily (73–71 BCE). Having served in the staff of another governor in 80 BCE, Verres had direct experience with the methods and rewards of tax revenue, so he tried to bypass the publicani. To be sure, his attempt had nothing to do with any sense of justice or with any regard for the provincials. Simply put, Verres wanted the entire pie for himself. When he arrived in Sicily, the socii of the main local company of publicani gathered to welcome him, surely in an attempt to establish a win-win partnership in crime. At first, Verres tried to collect the export tax without their help, but he was met by a firm reaction by the magistri, who governed the societas. These were capable businessmen, not easily taken in, so Verres compromised, and they collaborated.

Aside from requesting provincials to pay more than the legal 10 percent tax—that is, aside from supporting the typical abuses of the publicani—Verres proved creative. He added extra fees for inspections, collections, and exchanges; he even added an extra fee on sealing wax. Whether collectors reported to the publicani or directly to Verres, the number of cultivated acres would be inflated, hence placing absurd demands on Sicilian farmers such as Xeno and Polemarchus (selection 3) or on the people of Agyrium (selection 4). As a rule, an acre produced ten measures of grain; by law, then, farmers were expected to pay one measure of grain per each acre they farmed. Verres, however, asked for much more, accused farmers of declaring less land than they owned, and even sued them. The trouble is that, as governor, Verres was in charge of the courts. The provincials could appeal to Rome or just pay and hope for better times. Moreover, Verres's position allowed him to issue seemingly legal edicts to safeguard his machinations. In short, he made a fortune for himself and for his staff, and when he left Sicily, the societas of publicani seemed satisfied with his tenure as well. Clearly, they made more than they had invested.

The story does not end here. The Sicilians voiced complaints to Rome, and in 70 BCE Verres was tried for extortion. The plaintiffs faced an uphill battle. Verres was a senator, just like the judges who would cast the final verdict. His connections were perhaps even more impressive than his crimes. He was very close to the powerful family of the Metelli, which resembled a mafia clan, and he hired the best lawyer of his day, Hortensius. Hortensius had recently been elected to the highest magistracy in the Roman Republic, so he was slated to become one of the two consuls in 69 BCE. The other elected consul was Quintus Metellus. Quintus's younger brother Lucius Metellus, having succeeded Verres, was governor of Sicily. Obviously, Lucius could retort against the Sicilian provincials and hamper inquiries into his predecessor's crimes. The youngest brother, Marcus Metellus, was the judge presiding over the court where the case would be tried.

Verres must have felt untouchable, and perhaps he entered the court feeling as secure as Al Capone did in October 1931. But like Al Capone, he lost his case. The Sicilians hired a younger, up-and-coming lawyer—Cicero. Cicero collected an overwhelming amount of evidence against Verres and packaged it in powerful rhetoric, in a series of orations known as *Verrine Orations* or *In Verrem*. On the one hand, Cicero strategically avoided attacking or alienating the publicani (and hence the equestrian order); on the other hand, he reminded the panel of judges, which was composed of senators, that if they continued to cover up the appalling crimes of other senators, such as Verres, they might lose face. The senators realized that reduced credibility might force them to give up their exclusive right to judge in courts, and to share that right with the equestrian order. Verres was exiled. Cicero settled for such a low assessment of damages that some suspected he too had been corrupted. Still, the Sicilians celebrated the unexpected victory and showered Cicero with produce from their dear land.

Generations have read and loved the *Verrine Orations*, and there is no question that these orations deserve a special place in world prose. However, their reception is split on another account. Was it sense of justice or regard for their own convenience that led the senators to condemn a fellow senator?

Xenonis Menaeni, nobilissimi hominis, uxoris fundus erat colono locatus; colonus, quod decumanorum iniurias ferre non poterat, ex agro profugerat. Verres in Xenonem iudicium dabat illud suum damnatorium de iugerum professione. Xeno ad se pertinere negabat; fundum elocatum esse dicebat. Dabat iste iudicium, Si pareret ivgera eivs fvndi plvra esse qvam colonvs esset professvs, tum uti Xeno damnaretur. Dicebat ille non modo se non arasse, id quod satis erat, sed nec dominum eius esse fundi nec locatorem; uxoris esse; eam ipsam suum negotium gerere, ipsam locavisse. Defendebat Xenonem homo summo splendore et summa auctoritate praeditus, M. Cossutius. Iste nihilo minus iudicium HS iccc dabat. Ille tametsi recuperatores de cohorte latronum sibi parari videbat, tamen iudicium se accepturum esse dicebat. Tum iste maxima voce Veneriis imperat, ut Xeno audiret, dum res iudicetur hominem ut adservent; cum iudicata sit, ad se ut adducant; et illud simul ait, se non putare illum, si propter divitias poenam damnationis contemneret, etiam virgas contempturum. Hac ille vi et hoc metu adductus tantum decumanis dedit quantum iste imperavit.

Polemarchus est Murgentinus, vir bonus atque honestus. Ei cum pro iugeribus quinquaginta medimna dcc decumae imperarentur, quod recusabat, domum ad istum in ius eductus est, et, cum iste etiam cubaret,

3. THE MANY ABUSES BY VERRES, CICERO, VERRINE ORATIONS (IN VERREM) II 3.55–57

An estate belonging to the wife of the most noble Xeno Menaenius was contracted out to a farmer, but the farmer could not bear the abuses by tax collectors, so he stopped working the estate and ran off. Verres allowed legal proceedings to be opened against Xeno, who could be condemned on the usual charge of falsifying the number of cultivated acres. Xeno repeated that the charge did not apply to him, because the estate had been contracted out, but Verres conducted a trial to verify "whether it transpired that the acres of the estate were more than the farmer had declared," in which case Xeno should be condemned. Xeno declared not only that did he not work that estate, which by itself should have been enough to prevent a trial, but also that it was not he who owned or rented out the estate, but his wife. She conducted her business directly, and it was she who rented it out. Marcus Cossutius, a most dignified and respected man, defended Xeno, but Verres nevertheless allowed a fine of 50,000 sestertii. Xeno said that he would accept the verdict, even if he saw that the collectors were selected from Verres's gang of thieves. Then Verres cried in his loudest voice, so Xeno could hear, and ordered the slaves from the temple of Venus to keep Xeno in custody for the duration of the trials and to take Xeno to him after being sentenced. Verres added that, in his view, even if

in cubiculum introductus est, quod nisi mulieri et de-
cumano patebat alii nemini. Ibi cum pugnis et calcibus
concisus esset, qui dcc medimnis decidere noluisset,
mille promisit. Eubulidas est Grospus Centuripinus,
homo cum virtute et nobilitate domi suae, tum etiam
pecunia princeps. Huic homini, iudices, honestissimae
civitatis honestissimo non modo frumenti scitote sed
etiam vitae et sanguinis tantum relictum esse quantum
Aproni libido tulit; nam vi malo plagis adductus est ut
frumenti daret, non quantum deberet, sed quantum
cogeretur.

Sostratus et Numenius et Nymphodorus eiusdem
civitatis cum ex agris tres fratres consortes profugis-
sent, quod iis plus frumenti imperabatur quam quantum exararant, hominibus coactis in eorum arationes
Apronius venit, omne instrumentum diripuit, familiam abduxit, pecus abegit. Postea cum ad eum
Nymphodorus venisset Aetnam et oraret ut sibi sua
restituerentur, hominem corripi ac suspendi iussit in
oleastro quodam, quae est arbor, iudices, Aetnae in
foro. Tam diu pependit in arbore socius amicusque
populi Romani in sociorum urbe ac foro, colonus ara-
torque vester, quam diu voluntas Aproni tulit.

Xeno could shrug off the punishment of a fee, because he was so wealthy, he would be bothered by being scourged. So Xeno, forced by this violent threat, paid whatever portion of his harvest Verres asked.

Polemarchus is a good and honest man from Murgentia. He was asked to pay seven hundred measures of grain as a tax for five hundred acres of land. But he refused. He was dragged in judgment to Verres's house, and since Verres was still asleep, they led him into the bedroom, which was open to no one other than women and tax collectors. Here he was punched and kicked, so that even though he initially refused to pay seven hundred measures, he ended up promising one thousand. Eubilidas Grospus, from Centuripae, is outstanding for his virtue, nobility, and wealth. This man, members of the jury, this most honorable citizen of a most honorable town was left with as little grain, and even as little life and blood as it pleased Apronius. Indeed, with violence, mistreatment, and blows he was led to give whatever he was extorted, which was more than he owed.

From the same town come three brothers and co-owners, Sostratus, Numenius, and Nymphodorus. They fled from the fields because they were ordered to pay more grain than they produced. Apronius gathered some men and came to their fields. He destroyed all agricultural tools, took the slaves, and drove the cattle away. Then, Nymphodorus reached Verres at Aetna and asked him to return his property, but Verres

Ac primum de Agyrinensi populo fideli et inlustri breviter cognoscite. Agyrinensis est in primis honesta Siciliae civitas hominum ante hunc praetorem locupletium summorumque aratorum. Eius agri decumas cum emisset idem Apronius, Agyrium venit. Qui cum apparitoribus eo et vi ac minis venisset, poscere pecuniam grandem coepit ut accepto lucro discederet; nolle se negoti quicquam habere dicebat, sed accepta pecunia velle quam primum in aliam civitatem occurrere. Sunt omnes Siculi non contemnendi, si per nostros magistratus liceat, sed homines et satis fortes et plane frugi ac sobrii, et in primis haec civitas de qua loquor, iudices.

Itaque homini improbissimo respondent Agyrinenses sese decumas ei quem ad modum deberent daturos: lucrum, cum ille magno praesertim emisset, non addituros. Apronius certiorem facit istum cuia res erat. Statim, tamquam coniuratio aliqua Agyri contra rem publicam facta aut legatus praetoris pulsatus esset, ita Agyrio magistratus et quinque primi accitu istius evocantur. Veniunt Syracusas; praesto est Apronius;

had Nymphodorus arrested and hanged on a wild olive tree in the center of Aetna. So a friend and ally of the Roman people, a farmer who works for you, remained hanging in the center of an allied town for as long as Apronius wished.

4. MORE ABUSES BY VERRES, CICERO, VERRINE ORATIONS (IN VERREM) II 3.67–70

Before I begin, let me tell you a little about the loyal and distinguished people of Agyrium. Agyrium is one of the most respected towns of Sicily, with excellent farmers, who used to be wealthy — until Verres became governor. The above-mentioned Apronius obtained the right to collect the tithe in that region, so he came to Agyrium. After showing up with his servants, he began to threaten violence and requested a huge sum, promising that he would leave after he collected his money. "I'm not looking for trouble," he said, "and once I get the money I plan to move to the next town as soon as possible." No Sicilian should be regarded with contempt, if that's allowed by our governors; they are quite resolute, honest, and moderate, members of the jury, and this is particularly true of Agyrium.

And so the people of Agyrium responded to that most unjust individual that they would pay the fair tithe they owed but would not add the extra payment, especially since Apronius had already set a high tithe. Apronius informed Verres of the situation. At once,

ait eos ipsos qui venissent contra edictum praetoris fecisse. Quaerebant, quid? Respondebat se ad recuperatores esse dicturum. Iste aequissimus homo formidinem illam suam miseris Agyrinensibus iniciebat: recuperatores se de cohorte sua daturum minabatur. Agyrinenses, viri fortissimi, iudicio se passuros esse dicebant.

Ingerebat iste Artemidorum Cornelium medicum et Tlepolemum Cornelium pictorem et eius modi recuperatores, quorum civis Romanus nemo erat, sed Graeci sacrilegi iam pridem improbi, repente Cornelii. Videbant Agyrinenses, quicquid ad eos recuperatores Apronius attulisset, illum perfacile probaturum: condemnari cum istius invidia infamiaque malebant quam ad eius condiciones pactionesque accedere. Quaerebant quae in verba recuperatores daret. Respondebat, Si pareret adversvs edictvm fecisse; qua in re in iudicio dicturum esse aiebat. Iniquissimis verbis, improbissimis recuperatoribus conflictari malebant quam quicquam cum isto sua voluntate decidere. Summittebat iste Timarchidem qui moneret eos, si saperent, ut transigerent. Pernegabant. "Quid ergo? In singulos

as if a conspiracy against the state was formed at Agyrium, or as if an official of the governor had been beaten, the magistrates and five leading citizens from Agyrium were summoned by Verres. They came to Syracuse, and right away, Apronius accused them of violating an edict by the governor. "How so?" they asked, and he replied that he would say in the presence of his staff. Meanwhile Verres, the paradigm of justice, frightened those poor people, as he typically did. He threatened that he would assign Agyrium to *his* staff, but the people most courageously repeated that they were prepared to undergo a trial.

So Verres inflicted on them Artemidorus Cornelius, a doctor, and Tlepomenus Cornelius, a painter, and other collectors of that sort. None of them was a Roman citizen. They were Greek, sacrilegious, and longtime brigands. Then, out of nowhere, they became part of the family of the Cornelii. The people of Agyrium realized that Apronius could easily get away with whatever he demanded of those collectors, and yet they preferred to be condemned and give Verres an infamous name than stoop to the conditions of his deal. They asked according to which rule he had called in the collectors. He replied that "[the governor should call them in] if there was a clear violation of the edict" and added that he was going to speak about this in court. But they preferred to be tormented by those most unjust words and unfair collectors than accept any deal with him on his terms. Verres secretly sent

HS quinquagenis milibus damnari mavultis?" Malle dicebant. Tum iste clare omnibus audientibus, "Qui damnatus erit," inquit, "virgis ad necem caedetur." Hic illi flentes rogare atque orare coeperunt ut sibi suas segetes fructusque omnis arationesque vacuas Apronio tradere liceret, ut ipsi sine ignominia molestiaque discederent.

Hac lege, iudices, decumas vendidit Verres.

Timarchides to invite them to be wise and give in, but they flatly refused. "What then? Do you prefer to be condemned to pay 50,000 sestertii per person?" They repeated that they did, at which point Verres said clearly, while they were all listening, "whoever is fined will be clubbed to death." Here they broke into tears and began to pray and begged to be allowed to give Apronius their harvest, all their fruit, and the very fields and leave without suffering such dishonoring humiliation.

Men of the jury, this is how Verres allocated the collection of taxes.

Text 5. Introduction: A Spectacular Fraud by Two Publicani

In 212 BCE, the Second Punic War raged. Having crossed the Alps with a Carthaginian army, Hannibal devastated Italy. The Romans rose to the challenge and supported the military, but the situation remained critical. In the middle of this crisis, however, some publicani, loyal to their most terrible name, looked only for opportunities to profit. Marcus Postumius and Titus Pomponius won a public contract for shipping goods to Roman troops engaged on various fronts in the western Mediterranean. By contract, the state would bear the losses caused by storms. So these publicani loaded small and cheap cargo on old ships, sunk them, blamed the shipwreck on an accident, and filed for compensation, claiming that their cargo was more valuable than it actually had been.

The machination was discovered and brought to the attention of the senate. The senators, perhaps understandably, declined to take any action, fearing that they might alienate the powerful equestrian order, whose help they sorely needed. But the rumor was out, and Postumius, who must have been the main signatory of the contact, was sued by two plebeian tribunes who represented the Roman people. Postumius could rely on connections. He enjoyed the support of the equestrian order, to which he belonged, and Servilius, one of his relatives, being a plebeian tribune, had the power to veto the two other tribunes who had summoned him to court. In the case of a veto, the trial would be closed, and no verdict ever reached.

The court for noncapital offenses was formed by the entire tribal assembly (as seen in the trial of Furius Cresimus, described in chapter 1). Bits of text from various sources allow us to reconstruct the procedures of a Roman assembly. The magistrate conducting the prosecution—in this particular case, one of the tribunes—formally summoned the accused. On the day established for the trial, auspices would be taken by observing the flight of birds; if the auspices were favorable, the presiding magistrate would summon the other magistrates and the people. The assembly would formally begin with a prayer, and then the presider would introduce the case and bring in witnesses as needed. There would be room for some discussion, before a motion was put forth and officially read aloud by a herald. Next, an urn would be brought into the middle of the assembled crowd, and the tribunes would be allowed a final chance to veto the proceedings and end the assembly. Lots would be cast into the urn and drawn to determine both the order of voting and the tribe in which the Latins would vote (at this time, the Latins were not Roman citizens and did not belong to any tribe). Finally, each of the thirty-five tribes would express its vote, and the motion would be either accepted or rejected. Assemblies were quite loud and lively, with such cheering, clapping, and booing that, in most cases, the outcome of a discussion must have become clear before the votes were counted.

A large crowd gathered for Postumius's trial, and the regular procedure was followed in a tense climate. When the urn was brought in, the publicani started openly to pressure Servilius, the tribune and relative of Postumius, and urge him to use his veto and suspend the assembly; clearly, the motion and the popular feeling were leaning towards Postumius's condemnation. Servilius, however, could not withstand the pressure and resentment of the people, and the publicani resorted to violence. They closed ranks and charged toward the middle of the assembly, shouting at the tribunes and throwing everything into confusion. Roman assemblies had ended in riots before, and such carnage might have ensued now were it not for the intervention of Fulvius, who was one of the two consuls. Using his full authority, Fulvius invited the tribunes to dismiss the assembly. The assembly was dismissed, the people were dispersed, and the consuls summoned the senate to discuss what had happened. As typical, the senators argued from precedent. They examined previous occurrences wherein a powerful individual and the Roman people had crossed swords.

Hi, quia publicum periculum erat a vi tempestatis in iis quae portarentur ad exercitus et ementiti erant falsa naufragia et ea ipsa quae vera renuntiaverant fraude ipsorum facta erant, non casu. In veteres quassasque naves paucis et parvi pretii rebus impositis, cum mersissent eas in alto exceptis in praeparatas scaphas nautis, multiplices fuisse merces ementiebantur. Ea fraus indicata M. Aemilio praetori priore anno fuerat ac per eum ad senatum delata nec tamen ullo senatus consulto notata, quia patres ordinem publicanorum in tali tempore offensum nolebant.

Populus severior vindex fraudis erat; excitatique tandem duo tribuni plebis, Sp. et L. Carvilii, cum rem invisam infamemque cernerent, ducentum milium aeris multam M. Postumio dixerunt. Cui certandae cum dies advenisset conciliumque tam frequens plebis adesset ut multitudinem area Capitolii vix caperet, perorata causa una spes videbatur esse si C. Servilius Casca tribunus plebis, qui propinquus cognatusque Postumio erat, priusquam ad suffragium tribus vocarentur, intercessisset. Testibus datis tribuni populum submoverunt sitellaque lata est ut sortirentur ubi Latini suffragium ferrent. Interim publicani Cascae instare ut concilio diem eximeret; populus reclamare; et forte in cornu primus sedebat Casca, cui simul metus pudorque animum versabat. Cum in eo parum

5. *LIVY,* HISTORY OF ROME FROM ITS FOUNDATION *(AB URBE CONDITA) XXV 3–5*

Since the merchandise shipped to the army was covered by public insurance against storms, those two [Marcus Postumius of Pyrgi and Pomponius Veientanus] fabricated false shipwrecks, and the real shipwrecks that they reported were caused by their fraud, not by bad luck. In fact, they loaded small and inexpensive cargo on old and beaten ships. They sunk them in the deep, saved the sailors in lifeboats that they had prepared in advance, and then filed a claim for a huge cargo. In the previous year, this fraud was denounced to the praetor, Marcus Aemilius. He brought it to the attention of the senate, but the senate did not condemn it with any decree, because the senators did not want to upset the entire class of the publicans in the middle of such a deep crisis.

The Roman people, however, proved to be stricter in punishing the crime. An appeal was finally brought to two tribunes of the people, Spurius and Lucius Carvilius. Since they realized that this conduct was notoriously detested, they fined Postumius two hundred thousand bronze coins. On the day of the trial, the assembly of the people was so crowded that the entire area before the Capitol could barely hold them. The case was heard, and, clearly, the only hope left for Postumius depended on Servilius Casca, who was a tribune of the people and a close relative. As a tribune, he had the power to veto the entire trial before the people were called to vote tribe by tribe. The witnesses were heard,

praesidii esset, turbandae rei causa publicani per vacuum submoto locum cuneo inruperunt iurgantes simul cum populo tribunisque. Nec procul dimicatione res erat cum Fulvius consul tribunis "Nonne videtis, inquit, vos in ordinem coactos esse et rem ad seditionem spectare, ni propere dimittitis plebis concilium?"

Plebe dimissa senatus vocatur et consules referunt de concilio plebis turbato vi atque audacia publicanorum: M. Furium Camillum, cuius exsilium ruina urbis secutura fuerit, damnari se ab iratis civibus passum esse; decemviros ante eum, quorum legibus ad eam diem viverent, multos postea principes civitatis iudicium de se populi passos; Postumium Pyrgensem suffragium populo Romano extorsisse, concilium plebis sustulisse, tribunos in ordinem coegisse, contra populum Romanum aciem instruxisse, locum occupasse ut tribunos a plebe intercluderet, tribus in suffragium uocari prohiberet. Nihil aliud a caede ac dimicatione continuisse homines nisi patientiam magistratuum, quod cesserint in praesentia furori atque audaciae paucorum uincique se ac populum Romanum passi sint et comitia, quae reus ui atque armis prohibiturus erat, ne causa quaerentibus dimicationem daretur, voluntate ipsi sua sustulerint. Haec cum ab optimo quoque pro atrocitate rei accepta essent vimque eam contra rem publicam et pernicioso exemplo factam senatus decresset, confestim Carvilii tribuni plebis omissa multae certatione rei capitalis diem Postumio dixerunt ac

the tribunes made room in the middle of the crowd, and the urn was brought in to decide by lot to which tribe the Latini would cast their vote. Meanwhile, the publicans pressured Casca to veto the continuation of the assembly, and the people cried out against this. Casca happened to be sitting at the end of the bench, torn between fear and shame. The publicans realized that Casca would bring little help. So they lined up in a wedge and began to shout at the people and at the tribunes at once. They charged into the middle of the open area to throw the entire assembly into disorder. They came quite close to an open fight, when Fulvius, who was consul, told the tribunes, "Don't you see that you have been debased below your rank of tribunes? Don't you see that the situation will precipitate into an uproar, unless you dismiss this assembly of the people right now?"

The people dispersed, and the senate was summoned. The consuls reported that an assembly of the people had been thrown into confusion by the publicans' shameless recourse to violence. [Appealing to precedent,] they said that Marcus Furius Camillus allowed himself to be condemned by angered citizens, even if his exile could cause public ruin, and that before and after Camillus, the decemvirs, whose laws had lasted to that day, and many illustrious leaders had submitted to the people's judgment over them. Postumius of Pyrgi, however, tore the vote away from the Roman people. He disrupted an assembly of the people, debased the authority of the tribunes, and formed a battle line against the Roman people. He seized a position to cut

ni uades daret prendi a uiatore atque in carcerem duci iusserunt. Postumius vadibus datis non adfuit. Tribuni plebem rogaverunt plebesque ita scivit, si M. Postumius ante kalendas Maias non prodisset citatusque eo die non respondisset neque excusatus esset, videri eum in exsilio esse bonaque eius venire, ipsi aqua et igni placere interdici. Singulis deinde eorum qui turbae ac tumultus concitatores fuerant, rei capitalis diem dicere ac vades poscere coeperunt. Primo non dantes, deinde etiam eos qui dare possent in carcerem coniciebant; cuius rei periculum vitantes plerique in exsilium abierunt. Hunc fraus publicanorum, deinde fraudem audacia protegens exitum habuit.

off the tribunes from the people and prevented the tribes from casting their vote. Nothing checked a massive and deadly slaughter other than the magistrates' prudence. They temporarily yielded to the shameless madness of a few and allowed themselves and the Roman people to be defeated. To remove an excuse for rioting, they decided to dismiss the assembly, which the publicans had attempted to break up with violence and arms. The most respected citizens had endured all of this on account of the threatening situation, and the senate decided that it amounted to a dangerous precedent of violence against the state. Hence the Carvilii, who were tribunes of the plebs, on the spot put aside a proposal of a fine and summoned Postumius to court for capital punishment. They established that if he did not pay a deposit he should be captured by an officer and led into prison. Postumius paid the deposit but did not show up. The plebeian tribunes then made a motion to the popular assembly, and the people deliberated. If Marcus Postumius had not appeared by May 1, and if once summoned on that day he had not responded or was not excused, then he would be exiled. His possessions would be sold, and he should be sent into exile. Then they declared capital punishment for everyone who had agitated the crowd, and they began to ask for deposits. First, they threw into prison those who refused to pay and then even those who would. Most of them went spontaneously into exile to avoid this risk. The fraud by the publicans, and then a shameless attempt to cover it up, came to such an end.

Chapter 4

HOW TO INVEST, LOSE MONEY, AND GAIN POPULARITY

Giving Back to the People

Introduction

Toward the beginning of the second century CE, a poet named Juvenal famously remarked that there are only two things that the Roman people care about, bread and circuses. There is a lot of truth in this statement. It possibly reveals what the great majority of Romans wanted, and it certainly reveals how upper-class individuals, such as Juvenal, regarded the rest of the people.

The great majority of Romans received little benefit from the Empire and lived a life of poverty. Indeed, the growing power of Rome generated a widening gap between the rich and the poor, and as a result, the history of Rome is a tale of two cities. The urban mansions of the wealthy included splendid villas with porticoes, baths, pools, and gardens. These mansions stretched for acres and occupied invaluable real estate. The magnificence of these manors matched the magnificence of public buildings, such as temples, markets, circuses, and memorial monuments. All these buildings filled downtown Rome and occupied invaluable real estate as well.

Side by side, the remaining space belonged to the inhabitants of the other city. Here, every inch counted and was crowded by a mass of poor people, nameless to posterity. These individuals led a miserable life. Lack of public transportation forced them into narrow streets, where tall and ramshackle apartment buildings, called *insulae*, proliferated. It has been calculated that the population density in these areas of ancient Rome was comparable to modern Calcutta.

Insulae were not only crowded; they were also dangerous, filthy, and expensive. Typically, builders cut corners and erected insulae with cheaper sun-dried bricks, as kiln-baked bricks were reserved for those who could afford them. Landlords cut corners as well, investing no money in maintenance and even ignoring cracks in the structure. They were generally concerned only with cashing in on the rentals; however, they could avoid interacting with the renters and use go-between slaves to supervise an *insula* and collect the rent. Poor construction and lack of maintenance caused collapses, which were so frequent that the sound of falling buildings was not uncommon in Rome. Perhaps apartment renters, called *insularii*, feared fires even more than collapses, as a lack of light and heating led them to use candles and braziers.

Water was as badly supplied as light and heat, so that fires could spread quickly and destroy many insulae at once.

To fetch water for drinking and cooking, insularii walked to the closest fountain and then carried a full vessel back to their apartments. Since they did not have running water they obviously had no sinks, baths, or toilets. Those who could not pay the modest fee for public baths or latrines, along with those who found themselves too far away from such amenities, used chamber pots. Pots were emptied under the main stairs of an insula or, if a landlord did not allow that, at a neighboring dung heap. Many, however, simply emptied the pot out of the window, caring little for passersby. A person might be hit by flying excrement at any time, thus providing the rich yet another reason to avoid such areas. In case such a thing happened, lawyers shared tips on how to track down throwing offenders in a maze of crowded insulae.

All this luxury came at no modest price. Rentals in Rome were outrageously expensive, costing roughly four times as much as elsewhere. Since unskilled laborers could not afford them, they had to sublet, making insulae even more packed, dirty, and hazardous. These living conditions must have affected life expectancy. It has been estimated that roughly 30 percent of children died in their first year and that fewer than 50 percent survived their teens. On average, life expectancy was approximately twenty-seven to twenty-eight years.

These living conditions of the urban masses had other momentous consequences. Understandably, a great number of people lived outdoors as much as they could. They spent their time in the streets, rubbing shoulders with other insularii like themselves, and in forums, where they could rub shoulders with the wealthy as well. Second, extreme poverty made them quite sensitive to fluctuations in grain price and deeply dependent on free or heavily subsidized distributions. The unease of starvation—caused by an increase in grain price or a decline in imported goods—often escalated into outbursts of street riots.

The best way to contain these riots was to feed and entertain the people, that is, to offer them bread and circuses, as Juvenal puts it. During the Republic, leading magistrates or ambitious individuals offered food handouts, gladiatorial games, and other entertainment hoping to win popular favor and secure the votes they needed to advance their career. The Roman people duly rewarded generosity and creativity; for once, they were benefitting from the competition for power. This competition had one goal and one main rule: to one-up all past and present rivals. In 264 BCE, the year of the first recorded gladiatorial game, only three pairs of gladiators engaged in combat. It was a modest affair, but the numbers would increase dramatically. Sources record that twenty-two pairs fought in 216, twenty-five in 200, and sixty in 183. The numbers continued to increase, and pressure to win popular favor triggered the imagination of politicians. Some nobles attempted to curb the extravagance, likely because they could not keep up with the competition, and in 63 BCE, a law was passed to limit the maximum number of gladiators per show (see selection 3). But the law did not last, and roughly fifteen years later Caesar offered a show with one thousand fighters along with elephants and knights (as shown in selection 1).

Aside from the sponsor, various people benefitted from games, as they labored to provide transportation, food, lodging, and entertainment for crowds pouring in. Ancient inscriptions spell out various occupational categories, and many workers in these categories must have been directly affected by special events: animal tenders, baggage carriers, drivers, and boatmen relied on others' need for transportation; innkeepers provided lodging and food (along with prostitutes, as shown in chapter 6). However, visitors could find food in retail dealers, including grocery stores, bakeries, butcheries, and wine bars, and of course itinerant merchants sold fast food in the vicinity of circuses, theaters, and amphitheaters. A visit to the city provided plenty of opportunities for visitors in a mood for shopping, as well. Artisans who enjoyed a crowd of potential customers included jewelers, furriers, and gem cutters; makers of shoes, boots, and sandals; ironsmiths, silversmiths, and ivory carvers; makers of helmets, swords, and shields; tanners; and various retail dealers who specialized in wine bottles, honey, clothing and linens, and more.

Augustus, commonly considered the first Roman emperor, learned his Roman history lesson about how to please spectators and workers. Like Caesar, who was his adoptive father, Augustus spent lavishly on food distributions and spectacles, hence gaining a great deal of popular favor. But he wanted all such favor for himself. Accordingly, he begrudged anyone outside the imperial family from offering grain and public entertainment. Scooping out bread and circuses became the responsibility and exclusive right of emperors in Rome and of local magistrates supporting the emperors everywhere else. The numbers continued to grow. For example, in 80 CE, the Colosseum was inaugurated by the emperor Titus. For the opening games, five thousand beasts were slaughtered in animal hunts, and poetry by Martial (reported in selections 6–10) immortalized the festivities. In 107, Trajan celebrated a victorious campaign with ten thousand gladiators competing over 117 days of games offered to the people.

Texts 1–4. Introduction:
Caesar's Generosity, Debt, and Popularity

Given the centrality of "bread and circuses," the most successful politicians, such as Caesar and Augustus, were also the most lavish in cultivating popular favor. In selection 1, Suetonius lumps together gladiatorial games and grain distributions, demonstrating that these were different means to the same goal. Suetonius explains that Caesar offered an unprecedented variety of shows, including theatrical performances in different languages, chariot races, sea battles, athletic competitions, and a Trojan *lusus*, which was an equestrian event wherein noble youth showed off their riding skills. Caesar was particularly fond of gladiators. As a connoisseur and owner of a gladiatorial school, he selected his gladiators and carefully managed their training, as seen in selection 1. To support these performances, Caesar sustained astronomical expenses (as shown in selections 2 and 4), and he was up to his neck in debt. For example, to set up a naval battle, he had an artificial lake dug and brought in ships from fleets stationed in Lebanon and in Egypt. At the end, the investment all paid off. Swarms of visitors gathered to attend his shows and camped for days in tents; the crowds were so massive that some people were even crushed and suffocated.

Gladiatores notos, sicubi infestis spectatoribus dimi-
carent, vi rapiendos reservandosque mandabat. Tirones
neque in ludo neque per lanistas, sed in domibus per
equites Romanos atque etiam per senatores armorum
peritos erudiebat, precibus enitens, quod epistulis eius
ostenditur, ut disciplinam singulorum susciperent
ipsique dictata exercentibus darent. . . . Frumentum,
quotiens copia esset, etiam sine modo mensuraque
praebuit ac singula interdum mancipia e praeda viri-
tim dedit.

Edidit spectacula varii generis: munus gladiatorium, ludos etiam regionatim urbe tota et quidem per
omnium linguarum histriones, item circenses athle-
tas naumachiam. Munere in foro depugnavit Furius
Leptinus stirpe praetoria et Q. Calpenus senator
quondam actorque causarum. Pyrricham saltaverunt
Asiae Bithyniaeque principum liberi. Ludis Decimus
Laberius eques Romanus mimum suum egit dona-
tusque quingentis sestertiis et anulo aureo sessum in
quattuordecim [e] scaena per orchestram transiit. Cir-
censibus spatio circi ab utraque parte producto et in
gyrum euripo addito quadrigas bigasque et equos
desultorios agitaverunt nobilissimi iuvenes. Troiam
lusit turma duplex maiorum minorumque puerorum.

1. THE WIDE RANGE OF ENTERTAINMENT OFFERED BY CAESAR, SUETONIUS, LIFE OF JULIUS CAESAR (DIVUS IULIUS) 26 AND 39

If there were any famous gladiators that the crowd did not enjoy, Caesar recruited them forcibly from everywhere and retained them for himself. As for the apprentices, he did not have them coached in gladiatorial schools under professional trainers, but in private homes under Roman knights or even senators with military experience. He even begged them, as one can see from his letters, to undertake the education of these apprentices one on one and to supervise them as they practiced their exercises. . . . Whenever the grain abounded, he distributed without measure or limit, and more than once he donated one slave from the war booty to each of his soldiers.

Caesar sponsored different types of entertainments including: gladiatorial combats; theatrical performances, which were also staged in all the districts of the city—even with actors speaking in different languages; and finally chariot races, athletic competitions, and a sea battle. The gladiatorial shows took place in the Roman forum. Furius Leptinus, even though he came from a praetorian family, fought in these games as a gladiator, as did Quintus Calpenus, who used to be a senator and a lawyer. The children of princes from Asia Minor performed a

Venationes editae per dies quinque ac novissime pugna divisa in duas acies, quingenis peditibus, elephantis vicenis, tricenis equitibus hinc et inde commissis. Nam quo laxius dimicaretur, sublatae metae inque earum locum bina castra exadversum constituta erant. Athletae stadio ad tempus extructo regione Marti campi certaverunt per triduum. Navali proelio in minore Codeta defosso lacu biremes ac triremes quadriremesque Tyriae et Aegyptiae classis magno pugnatorum numero conflixerunt. Ad quae omnia spectacula tantum undique confluxit hominum, ut plerique advenae aut inter vicos aut inter vias tabernaculis positis manerent, ac saepe prae turba elisi exanimatique sint plurimi et in his duo senatores.

Pyrrhic dance. As part of the theatrical events, Decimus Laberius, who was a Roman knight, performed a mime he had composed. He received a gift of 500 sestertii and a gold ring; then he left the stage, walked across the orchestra, and sat in one of the fourteen benches reserved for knights. For the chariot races, Caesar added room to both sides of the circuit and dug a ditch around it. The most noble youth competed in races with two- and with four-horse chariots and hopped from one galloping horse to another. A squadron of junior and senior boys on horseback performed the Trojan lusus. Animal hunts lasted for five days. On the last day, there was a battle with one thousand soldiers divided into two armies, with twenty elephants and thirty knights each. On that occasion, to create more space for the battle, Caesar replaced the turning posts used for chariot races with two camps facing each other. Athletes competed for three days in a circuit built for the occasion in the area of the Campus Martius. The sea battle took place in a lake dug near the Field of Mars: warships with two, three, and four banks of oars were taken from the fleet at Tyro and from Egypt, and a great number of sailors took part in the fight. Such a great number of spectators from everywhere gathered for all these shows that many visitors lodged in tents in the city streets. More than once, many were crushed and suffocated by the crowd, including two senators.

χρώμενος δὲ ταῖς δαπάναις ἀφειδῶς, καὶ δοκῶν μὲν ἐφήμερον καὶ βραχεῖαν ἀντικαταλλάττεσθαι μεγάλων ἀναλωμάτων δόξαν, ὠνούμενος δὲ ταῖς ἀληθείαις τὰ μέγιστα μικρῶν, λέγεται πρὶν εἰς ἀρχήν τινα καθίστασθαι χιλίων καὶ τριακοσίων γενέσθαι χρεωφειλέτης ταλάντων. ἐπεὶ δὲ τοῦτο μὲν ὁδοῦ τῆς Ἀππίας ἀποδειχθεὶς ἐπιμελητὴς πάμπολλα χρήματα προσανάλωσε τῶν ἑαυτοῦ, τοῦτο δὲ ἀγορανομῶν ζεύγη μονομάχων τριακόσια καὶ εἴκοσι παρέσχε καὶ ταῖς ἄλλαις περὶ θέατρα καὶ πομπὰς καὶ δεῖπνα χορηγίαις καὶ πολυτελείαις τὰς πρὸ αὐτοῦ κατέκλυσε φιλοτιμίας, οὕτω διέθηκε τὸν δῆμον ὡς καινὰς μὲν ἀρχὰς καινὰς δὲ τιμὰς ζητεῖν ἕκαστον, αἷς αὐτὸν ἀμείψαιντο.

Et nos fecimus quae posteri fabulosa arbitrentur. Caesar, qui postea dictator fuit, primus in aedilitate munere patris funebri omni apparatu harenae argenteo usus est, ferasque etiam argenteis vasis incessivere tum primum noxii, quod iam etiam in municipiis aemulantur.

2. CAESAR'S INVESTMENT, PLUTARCH, LIFE OF CAESAR (ΚΑΙΣΑΡ) 5

Caesar spent an incredible amount of money, and it seemed that he gained back only short-lived favor for the huge sums he had spent. But in truth, he was acquiring much with little. Apparently, before holding any public office, he had already accumulated a debt for 1,300 talents. Then, when he was elected to be the curator of the Appian way, he spent much out of his own pocket, and when he became aedile he put on a show with 320 pairs of gladiators. With other extravagant expenditures for theatrical performances, processions, and meals, he overshadowed the generosity of his predecessors. In this way, he so disposed the people that everyone demanded new magistracies and honors to repay him.

3. CAESAR'S EXTRAVAGANCE, ELDER PLINY, NATURAL HISTORY (NATURALIS HISTORIA) XXXIII 16.53

Future generations will count as legendary some of our endeavors. As an aedile and before becoming a dictator, Caesar was the first one to use only silver powder for sand in the funeral gladiatorial games he hosted for his father. That was also the first time when convicted criminals wore silver equipment to fight wild beasts, a practice that is now imitated even in towns outside Rome.

Texts 4 and 5. Introduction: Making Generosity Known and Remembered

Once free grain distributions or some exciting entertainment were announced, word of mouth would quickly spread the news. Heralds would make public announcements in forums, where the people gathered, and graffiti spelled out the details for those who could read. Whatever was offered to the people would be quickly gobbled up. But this was not the end of the story for a sponsor. Sponsors invested huge sums of money, often incurring debt in order to make a splash. Hence, they needed to advertise, and they were especially worried about attaching their name to an event. Selection 4 includes two graffiti from Pompeii. The first advertises a gladiatorial show (and its sponsor's name). It provides all the needed details without specifying the location, because everyone knew that gladiators competed in the local amphitheater. The second promotes the candidature of a certain Marcus Casellius Marcellus promising that, as a good aedile, he would invest in entertainment.

Selection 5 comes from emperor Augustus's *Res gestae* (*Personal Achievements*). Toward the end of his life, Augustus wrote a self-advertising story of his deeds. This story highlights his unparalleled generosity toward the Roman people, and Augustus had reason to brag. He restored decaying temples, roads, aqueducts, and bridges; he generously sponsored public constructions, including new temples, a new forum, and a theater; he donated a massive amount of money, and—of course—he sponsored spectacular entertainment events. Nothing suggests that Augustus personally enjoyed gladiatorial games, as Caesar did, but every piece of evidence shows that Augustus had learned how to earn and maintain the support of the masses.

The contents of *Res gestae* were read in the first senatorial meeting after Augustus's death. They were also inscribed in bronze and placed on his tomb, the Mausoleum, which had been completed in 28 BCE, almost five decades before Augustus wrote about his achievements and died in 14 CE. Bronze was a durable material that carried an aura of sacred authority, since Romans used it for laws and official documents. These tablets, however, did not last, as over the centuries the bronze must have been melted to be reused. Selection 5 reproduces the Latin text from one of the three copies of the inscription we have. The copy was found on the temple of Rome and Augustus in Ankara, Turkey. Thanks to their length, good preservation, and historical importance, the *Res gestae* is known as "the queen of inscriptions." The significance of the *Res gestae* is beyond dispute, but Augustus did not have Caesar's literary genius. His Latin is clear but inelegant, and at times even dull and boring.

A(vli) Svetti Certi / aedilis familia gladiatoria pvgnab(it) Pompeis / pr(idie) Kalendas Ivnias venatio et vela ervnt

M(arcvm) Casellivm Marcellvm aedilem bonvm et mvnerarivm magnvm

Capitolium et Pompeium theatrum utrumque opus impensa grandi refeci sine ulla inscriptione nominis mei. Rivos aquarum compluribus locis vetustate labentes refeci, et aquam quae Marcia appellatur duplicavi fonte novo in rivum eius inmisso. Forum Iulium et basilicam quae fuit inter aedem Castoris et aedem Saturni, coepta profligataque opera a patre meo, perfeci et eandem basilicam consumptam incendio, ampliato eius solo, sub titulo nominis filiorum meorum incohavi, et, si vivus non perfecissem, perfici ab heredibus meis iussi. Duo et octoginta templa deum in urbe consul sextum ex auctoritate senatus refeci nullo praetermisso quod eo tempore refici debebat. Consul septimum viam Flaminiam ab urbe Ariminum refeci pontesque omnes praeter Mulvium et Minucium.

4. TWO ADS FOR GAMES IN POMPEII, CORPUS OF LATIN INSCRIPTIONS (CORPUS INSCRIPTIONUM LATINARUM) IV 1189 AND 4.4999

The gladiatorial school of the aedile Aulus Suettius Certus will fight in Pompeii on May 31; [the show will include] an animal hunt and blinds for shade.

Marcus Casellius Marcellus, a good aedile and generous sponsor of games.

5. SELF-PROCLAIMED ACCOMPLISHMENTS, AUGUSTUS, PERSONAL ACHIEVEMENTS (RES GESTAE) 20–22

I restored the Capitol and the Theater of Pompey. Both were quite expensive, and I didn't take the credit with a commemorative inscription in either case. In many locations I rebuilt aqueducts that were falling apart because of old age. I doubled the output of the pool, known as "Aqua Marcia," by drawing on the river through another channel. I completed the forum and the basilica Iulia, which my [adoptive] father [Julius Caesar] had started and almost finished, and which is located between the temples of Castor and Saturn. I restored the same basilica as well, after it was damaged by fire; I increased its size. I began the restoration with an inscription in the name of my sons, and in the event that I should die before completing it, I ordered that it should be completed by my

In privato solo Martis Ultoris templum forumque Augustum ex manibiis feci. Theatrum ad aedem Apollinis in solo magna ex parte a privatis empto feci, quod sub nomine M. Marcelli generi mei esset. Dona ex manibiis in Capitolio et in aede divi Iuli et in aede Apollinis et in aede Vestae et in templo Martis Ultoris consacravi, quae mihi constiterunt HS circiter milliens. Auri coronari pondo triginta et quinque millia municipiis et colonis Italiae conferentibus ad triumphos meos quintum consul remisi, et postea, quotienscumque imperator appellatus sum, aurum coronarium non accepi decernentibus municipiis et colonis aeque benigne atque antea decreverant.

Ter munus gladiatorium dedi meo nomine et quinquiens filiorum meorum aut nepotum nomine, quibus muneribus depugnaverunt hominum circiter decem millia. Bis athletarum undique accitorum spectaculum populo praebui meo nomine et tertium nepotis mei nomine. Ludos feci meo nomine quater, aliorum autem magistratuum vicem ter et viciens. Pro conlegio XV virorum magister conlegii collega M. Agrippa ludos saeclares C. Furnio C. Silano cos. feci. Consul XIII ludos Martiales primus feci quos post id tempus deinceps insequentibus annis s.c. et lege fecerunt consules. Venationes bestiarum Africanarum meo nomine aut filiorum meorum et nepotum in circo aut in foro aut in amphitheatris populo dedi sexiens et viciens, quibus confecta sunt bestiarum circiter tria millia et quingentae.

successors. In my sixth consulship I rebuilt eighty-two temples in Rome, by decree of the senate, and at that time I did not overlook any temple that needed repair. In my seventh consulship, I redid the Flaminian way from Rimini, including all the bridges, but the Milvian and the Minucian.

I erected the temple of Mars the Avenger and the Forum of Augustus on my private land and paid for them by war booty. I constructed a theater next to the temple of Apollo on land I purchased mostly from individuals. I wanted this temple to be dedicated by my son-in-law, Marcus Marcellus. I consecrated war booty in the Capitol and in the temples of Divine Julius, of Apollo, of Vesta, and of Mars the Avenger, for a total of about 100 million sestertii. In my fifth consulship, I returned the thirty-five thousand pounds of crown gold, which the Italian towns and colonies offered for my triumphs. Later, whenever I was saluted as a victorious general, I did not accept crown gold, even if the towns and provinces were presenting it as generously as they had in the past.

Three times I sponsored gladiatorial shows in my own name, and five times in the name of my sons or grandsons. About ten thousand gladiators fought in these shows. I provided competitions for the people, with athletes from all over, twice in my own name, and a third time in that of my grandson. I organized games, four times in my name and twenty-three times in the name of other magistrates. During the consulship of

Furnius and Silanus, I acted on behalf of the college of Fifteen; as master of this college with my colleague Marcus Agrippa, I promoted the Century games. In my thirteenth consulship, I was first to organize the games of Mars, and since then the consuls by decree of the senate and by law organize it annually. I sponsored hunts for the people with animals from Africa in my own name or of my sons or of my grandsons. I organized those in the circus or in the forum or in amphitheaters a total of twenty-six times. In these hunts, about three thousand five hundred beasts were killed.

Texts 6–10. Introduction:
Some Poems Celebrating the
Inauguration of the Colosseum

Popular spectacles were offered in Rome centuries before permanent structures were built to host them. Between 264 BCE, the year of the first recorded gladiatorial performance, and 29 BCE, when the first permanent amphitheater was inaugurated, Romans would construct temporary wooden buildings for these games. After a few days' use, these buildings would be dismantled. Following a similar pattern, the first recorded theatrical show took place in 364 BCE, but no permanent theater was built in Rome until 55 BCE. The project of erecting from scratch a new theater or amphitheater, with the capacity to seat

thousands of people, must have added to the spectators' excitement for the event. The procedure, however, was highly impractical and dramatically raised
the expenses of entertainment for the sponsors; still,
it created an opportunity for more workers, such as
architects, engineers, woodcutters, smiths, builders,
sculptors, carvers, painters, and various other contractors. For example, in 58 BCE, Aemilius Scaurus built a
theater with an enormous stage, fully adorned with
columns and with three thousand bronze statues. The
senate, however, strongly opposed permanent theaters
and amphitheaters, allegedly out of concern for public
morality. The senators might have also been motivated
by the fear that stable buildings may foster popular seditions or one individual might win everlasting favor
by attaching his name to a permanent construction.

In 80 CE, Rome finally gained its most famous amphitheater, the massive Colosseum. In less than ten
years, the Romans erected the impressive structure we
can still admire to this day. The Colosseum reaches a
height of 150 feet and could seat roughly fifty thousand spectators. People accessed the sitting area, called
the *cavea*, through eighty gates, which gave access to
four separated regions reserved respectively for the
imperial family, other political authorities, the knights,
and the commoners. A few years after its inauguration, a maze of tunnels was added underneath the
arena (which is Latin for "sand"), where gladiators
fought. Wild beasts entered the arena through these

tunnels, by means of a system of elevators activated by winches.

Titus, who was emperor in 80 CE, inaugurated the Colosseum with one hundred days of games and with distributions of gifts, including free grain. In the same year a clever poet, named Martial, composed some epigrams to celebrate this inauguration. Selections 6–10 come from a collection of these epigrams, called *Liber de spectaculis*, or *Book of Spectacles*. According to the literary convention of the genre, epigrams are short and witty. In particular, the epigrams from the *Book of Spectacles* give a vivid sense both of the pride caused by the construction of the Colosseum and of the widespread excitement elicited by the inaugural games (see selection 6). The next three epigrams are ecstatic commentaries on the inaugural games. Selection 7 celebrates an animal hunt, and selections 8 and 9 praise a naval battle and a gladiatorial combat. They show that games had to amaze the spectators in order to win their favor and cultivate their loyalty. But celebrating games could help to make money as well; Titus appreciated the charm and wit of Martial's verses, and he rewarded the poet with a generous gift.

The last epigram celebrates the favorable location of the Colosseum. It replaced the lavish mansions that used to belong to Nero and stood next to the "Colossus" (a massive statue of Nero from which the amphitheater took its name). Martial praises Titus's choice of location, observing that the space that "arrogant

Nero" had taken for himself had finally been returned to the people. This statement holds partially true. Out of the eighty gates giving access into the Colosseum, two were reserved for the imperial family, and forty-eight for the commoners. Different entrances led to the same place, and the tale of two cities ended in the amphitheater, where emperors and insularii came together to celebrate Rome. The executions of criminals symbolized the triumph of Roman justice; wild animals documented the variety of the lands Romans had conquered; the fights reenacted foreign victories, and the people pressed the emperors to grant life or death to a struggling gladiator. A wise emperor put the power of Rome on display before the eyes of the masses, and for a moment they might have felt that they held the helm. Maybe they cared about nothing but bread and circuses. Or perhaps these were the very few assets of the Empire that did not fall beyond their reach.

Barbara pyramidum sileat miracula Memphis,
    Assyrius iactet nec Babylona labor;
nec Triuiae templo molles laudentur Iones,
    dissimulet Delon cornibus ara frequens
aere nec uacuo pendentia Mausolea   5
    laudibus inmodicis Cares in astra ferant.
Omnis Caesareo cedit labor Amphitheatro,
    unum pro cunctis fama loquetur opus.

Summa tuae, Meleagre, fuit quae gloria famae,
    quantast Carpophori portio, fusus aper!
Ille et praecipiti uenabula condidit urso,
    primus in Arctoi qui fuit arce poli,
strauit et ignota spectandum mole leonem,   5
    herculeas potuit qui decuisse manus,
et uolucrem longo porrexit uulnere pardum.
    Praemia cum tandem ferret, adhuc poterat.

6. THE UNSURPASSED MARVEL OF THE COLOSSEUM, MARTIAL, BOOK OF SPECTACLES (LIBER DE SPECTACULIS) 1

Let barbarian Memphis fall silent about the marvels of the pyramids; let the Assyrian laborer not boast about building Babylon; let the effeminate Ionians not be praised for the temple of Trivia; let the altar covered with horns leave Delos unnoticed; and let the Carians not pile up excessive praises and extoll to the stars their suspended Mausoleum. Each of these buildings yields to the Amphitheater built by our emperor. Let fame proclaim this building alone instead of all of those.

7. A HUNTER WORTHY OF THE COLOSSEUM, MARTIAL, BOOK OF SPECTACLES (LIBER DE SPECTACULIS) 15

Meleagrus, your highest glory and fame for hunting a boar is only a fraction of Carpophorus's. He also sunk a spear into the fiercest bear in the Arctic, who rushed against him; he struck down a lion of such unprecedented size that it could have been a match for Hercules; he hit a running leopard from a distance. At the end, when he received his reward, he still had energy left.

Si quis ades longis serus spectator ab oris,
    cui lux prima sacri muneris ista fuit,
ne te decipiat ratibus naualis Enyo
    et par unda fretis, hic modo terra fuit.
Non credis? Specta, dum lassant aequora Martem: 5
    parua mora est, dices 'Hic modo pontus erat.'

Cum traheret Priscus, traheret certamina Verus,
    esset et aequalis Mars utriusque diu,
missio saepe uiris magno clamore petita est;
    sed Caesar legi paruit ipse suae;—
lex erat, ad digitum posita concurrere parma: 5
    quod licuit, lances donaque saepe dedit.
Inuentus tamen est finis discriminis aequi:
    pugnauere pares, subcubuere pares.
Misit utrique rudes et palmas Caesar utrique:
    hoc pretium uirtus ingeniosa tulit.   10
Contigit hoc nullo nisi te sub principe, Caesar:
    cum duo pugnarent, uictor uterque fuit.

8. THE VERSATILITY OF THE COLOSSEUM, MARTIAL, BOOK OF SPECTACLES (LIBER DE SPECTACULIS) 24

If you arrive here late as a spectator from far away, and if this is the first time you are witnessing Roman holy games, do not be deceived by the naval battle with warships; do not be deceived by the waves that match those of the sea. Just a moment ago, there was land here. You do not believe me? Just wait for the battle on water to settle. Very soon you will say "there was just an ocean here!"

9. A LONG GLADIATORIAL COMBAT WITH AN UNEXPECTED END, MARTIAL, BOOK OF SPECTACLES (LIBER DE SPECTACULIS) 29

Priscus and Verus kept dragging out the combat. For a long while, this fight remained equally balanced, so the people loudly and repeatedly asked that both gladiators be spared. But the emperor adhered to the rule he himself had established: "let a fight end only when a shield is dropped and a finger raised." More than once, he lawfully gave them gifts, precious dishes, and presents [but the combat went on]. At the end, a proper conclusion for this balanced fight was found. They fought equally and equally they surrendered. Caesar spared both, gave each a staff of victory and a palm of retirement. This was the reward for their courage and skill. This had never happened before, emperor: that two gladiators fought and both won.

Hic ubi sidereus propius uidet astra colossus
    et crescunt media pegmata celsa uia,
inuidiosa feri radiabant atria regis
    unaque iam tota stabat in urbe domus;
hic ubi conspicui uenerabilis Amphitheatri   5
    erigitur moles, stagna Neronis erant;
hic ubi miramur uelocia munera thermas,
    abstulerat miseris tecta superbus ager;
Claudia diffusas ubi porticus explicat umbras,
    ultima pars aulae deficientis erat.   10
Reddita Roma sibi est et sunt te preside, Caesar,
    deliciae populi, quae fuerant domini.

10. ROME RETURNED TO HERSELF, MARTIAL, BOOK OF SPECTACLES (LIBER DE SPECTACULIS) 2

Here the colossal statue [of Nero] enjoys a closer look at the stars, and giant cranes grow higher and higher in the middle of the street. This is the place where the hateful halls of the cruel tyrant [Nero] used to glitter, and a single house stretched out over all of Rome. Here the majestic mass of the huge Amphitheater rises from where Nero's lake used to be. Here we marvel at the public baths and how quickly they were completed, where the property of arrogant Nero had deprived the poor people of their homes. The colonnade of Claudia now extends its prolonged shade where the furthest part of Nero's house used to be. Rome is being returned to herself, and under your rule, emperor, what used to delight a single master now delights all people.

Chapter 5

HOW TO INVEST AND LOSE MONEY, POPULARITY, AND EVERYTHING ELSE

Disastrous Investments

Introduction

As with all investments, sponsoring games involved some risk and required careful planning. To host a gladiatorial show, a sponsor would first approach a *lanista* (plural *lanistae*), the manager of a school where gladiators lived and trained. As with modern sport teams, schools were ranked according to their fame and quality. The more famous the school, the higher the price a sponsor would be expected to pay. For this reason, some graffiti in Pompeii advertise a show by naming the school whence the gladiators were rented. People knew what it meant. Having chosen a school, a sponsor (or someone from his staff) would approach the lanista and negotiate a deal. The two would sign a contract spelling out the specific details, such as the length of the show, the number and type of gladiators and combats, and whether the combatants would fight to the death. In cases of life and death, the price went up. Offering a show with cheap gladiators might backfire and elicit popular resentment rather than gratitude. Moreover, as seen in chapter 4, unless a local amphitheater was available, sponsors would have to build one. This meant finding and transporting good wood and hiring architects, engineers, and a great number of laborers. Cutting corners on the construction of a facility could backfire as well, as shown in selection 2.

To make an impression, sponsors could combine gladiatorial fights, which were typically offered in the afternoon, and animal hunts, typically offered in the morning. A letter written to Cicero by his friend Caelius offers a glimpse into the complexities of animal hunting and trafficking for entertainment. In 51–50 BCE, Cicero was the governor of Cilicia, a province in modern southeast Turkey. Caelius candidly wrote that he needed some leopards to launch his political career; he pressed his request because Curio, one of his main competitors, had succeeded in obtaining exotic animals from his friends who were also governors. Offering a show with fewer and less exotic animals would fail to impress the crowds. Similarly, a few years before Caelius wrote to Cicero, the masses felt cheated at being presented with animals they had already seen many times. As we will see in selection 1, the masses were quite willing to express their disappointment at a subpar performance. They desired more and newer excitement.

DISASTROUS INVESTMENTS

Investing cheaply or badly in entertainment was not the only way one could lose both money and popularity. Generals leading a campaign enjoyed great freedom in disposing of the war booty, so they could win or lose big. Depending on their success and munificence, soldiers could win or lose as well. For this reason, the poet Catullus complains about enrolling under a useless general, as shown in selection 6. He envies those who followed Caesar in Gaul and pokes fun at two friends who fared as poorly as he did. Finally, selections 3–5 document the spectacular career of Crassus, one of the most successful businessmen in the Roman Republic. His last investment, however, turned out to be a stunning failure for generals and soldiers alike.

FAILED ENTERTAINMENTS

Texts 1 and 2. Introduction: Failed Entertainments

In 55 BCE, Pompey inaugurated the first permanent theater ever built in Rome. The opening ceremonies were to include dramatic performances, gladiatorial combats, and animal hunts. Expectations were high, and Cicero went as far as declaring that the magnificent show offered by Pompey would be unimaginable for the present and inimitable for posterity. No one wanted to miss the big event. A certain Marius, however, was out of town and asked Cicero to send a written account of the games and some consolation for missing them. Cicero complied, and his reply to Marius is reproduced in selection 1. Cicero elegantly articulates some quasi-philosophical reasons why one should scorn the games he had just attended. Then he quickly launches into a list of what went wrong. Cicero was not alone in feeling disappointed, as apparently the masses were dissatisfied as well, and Pompey admitted that the performances fell below expectations. Cicero's letter, then, demonstrates that investing in games could be a risky business. Pompey's popularity declined; just a few months after the inauguration, the people elected Domitius and Cato to the highest magistracies. They were Pompey's worst enemies.

Under Augustus's reign, the imperial family began to take charge of offering games in Rome, but local communities still relied on individual generosity (and on individual ambition). Accordingly, in 27 CE, a certain Atilius undertook the construction of an amphitheater to host gladiatorial shows in Fidenae. Large masses gathered to watch the games, both because the small town of Fidenae was just eight miles north of Rome, and because such games were a rare commodity under the emperor Tiberius, who disliked gladiatorial combats. Atilius's games turned out even worse than Pompey's.

Si te dolor aliqui corporis aut infirmitas valetudinis tuae tenuit, quo minus ad ludos venires, fortunae magis tribuo quam sapientiae tuae; sin haec, quae ceteri mirantur, contemnenda duxisti et, cum per valetudinem posses, venire tamen noluisti, utrumque laetor, et sine dolore corporis te fuisse et animo valuisse, cum ea, quae sine causa mirantur alii, neglexeris, modo ut tibi constiterit fructus otii tui, quo quidem tibi perfrui mirifice licuit, cum esses in ista amoenitate paene solus relictus. Neque tamen dubito, quin tu in illo cubiculo tuo, ex quo tibi Stabianum perforasti et patefecisti Misenum, per eos dies matutina tempora lectiunculis consumpseris, cum illi interea, qui te istic reliquerunt, spectarent communes mimos semisomni. . . .

Extremus elephantorum dies fuit: in quo admiratio magna vulgi atque turbae, delectatio nulla exstitit; quin etiam misericordia quaedam consecuta est atque opinio eiusmodi, esse quandam illi beluae cum genere humano societatem.

FAILED ENTERTAINMENTS

1. DÉJÀ-VU, OR HOW TO DISAPPOINT, CICERO, LETTERS TO HIS FRIENDS (EPISTULAE AD FAMILIARES) VII 1, EXCERPTS

If it was some indisposition that prevented you from coming to the shows, then I credit it to good luck more than to your wisdom. But if you despised the games that other people admire and decided not to come even though you were well, then I am happy for two reasons: because you were sound in your body and judgment alike, and because you looked down on what others approve without a reason. As a result, you enjoyed your free time, and indeed you were able to really enjoy it, because you were left practically alone in your delightful estate. No doubt, you got to spend your mornings reading in your wonderful bedroom, from which you enjoy the view of the Stabianum and of Misenum. Meanwhile, the other people who left you behind were watching some boring mimes half asleep. . . .

The last day was reserved for elephants. The mass of people was amazed but did not enjoy this. On the contrary, they felt a sort of compassion and a sense that these beasts have something in common with human beings.

M. Licinio L. Calpurnio consulibus ingentium bellorum cladem aequavit malum improvisum: eius initium simul et finis extitit. Nam coepto apud Fidenam amphitheatro Atilius quidam libertini generis, quo spectaculum gladiatorum celebraret, neque fundamenta per solidum subdidit neque firmis nexibus ligneam compagem superstruxit, ut qui non abundantia pecuniae nec municipali ambitione sed in sordidam mercedem id negotium quaesivisset. Adfluxere avidi talium, imperitante Tiberio procul voluptatibus habiti, virile ac muliebre secus, omnis aetas, ob propinquitatem loci effusius; unde gravior pestis fuit, conferta mole, dein convulsa, dum ruit intus aut in exteriora effunditur immensamque vim mortalium, spectaculo intentos aut qui circum adstabant, praeceps trahit atque operit.

Et illi quidem quos principium stragis in mortem adflixerat, ut tali sorte, cruciatum effugere: miserandi magis quos abrupta parte corporis nondum vita deseruerat; qui per diem visu, per noctem ululatibus et gemitu coniuges aut liberos noscebant. Iam ceteri fama exciti, hic fratrem, propinquum ille, alius parentes lamentari. Etiam quorum diversa de causa amici aut necessarii aberant, pavere tamen; nequedum comperto quos illa vis perculisset, latior ex incerto metus.

2. A SPECTACLE OF DISGRACE, TACITUS, ANNALS (ANNALES) IV 62–63

Under the consulship of Marcus Licinius and Lucius Calpurnius [in 27 CE], a tragedy suddenly struck, and it was so big that it matched the disasters caused by great wars. The tragedy started and ended at once. A certain Atilius, who was the son of a freedman, began constructing an amphitheater for gladiatorial games at Fidenae. But he did not cast the foundations into solid land, and he built the wooden structure on loose joints. He wanted to offer games as a base means to make money, not because he already had plenty or because he wanted to advance his public career. People with an appetite for games, deprived of this type of entertainment by the emperor Tiberius, came from everywhere, men and women of different ages. There was a great turnout because Fidenae is close to Rome. For this reason, the disaster was more lethal. The construction turned in on itself, then it shattered and collapsed. It pulled down and crushed an immense multitude of people, both those who were inside watching the shows and those who were gathered around the building.

Some met their fate at the beginning of the collapse. Even with such an end, at least they were spared further suffering. Even more miserable were those who were mutilated and remained alive. Those who tried to find spouses and children by sight during the day

Vt coepere dimoveri obruta, concursus ad exanimos complectentium, osculantium; et saepe certamen si confusior facies sed par forma aut aetas errorem adgnoscentibus fecerat. Quinquaginta hominum milia eo casu debilitata vel obtrita sunt; cautumque in posterum senatus consulto ne quis gladiatorium munus ederet cui minor quadringentorum milium res neve amphitheatrum imponeretur nisi solo firmitatis spectatae. Atilius in exilium actus est. Ceterum sub recentem cladem patuere procerum domus, fomenta et medici passim praebiti, fuitque urbs per illos dies quamquam maesta facie veterum institutis similis, qui magna post proelia saucios largitione et cura sustentabant.

and by shouts and groans after dark were equally miserable. The other ones, summoned by the news, gathered there and mourned a brother, a relative, or parents. Still others had friends or relatives away for another reason but were terrorized nevertheless. And until they had identified the victims, the lack of information produced yet more fear.

As soon as they started to clear the debris, people rushed to hug and kiss the dead bodies. At times they even argued because a face might be disfigured, or similar in shape and age [to another's victim] and it would cause the rescuers to make a mistake. Fifty thousand people were mutilated or killed in that disaster. The senate decreed that, from then on, gladiatorial shows could be offered only by individuals with a minimum patrimony of 400 thousand sesterces, and that amphitheaters could be built only on ground of proven stability. Atilius was exiled. Immediately after the disaster, wealthy citizens opened their homes to provide medicine and doctors in various places. The city was in mourning at this time, and yet it looked like the good old days, when after a major battle everyone helped out the wounded with generosity and care.

Texts 3 and 4. Introduction: How to Lose Everything

Marcus Licinius Crassus (115–53 BCE) had a lot of good qualities. He was extremely wealthy but kept a moderate lifestyle; he cared about his family and treated women and slaves better than most of his peers did; he dined with ordinary people and welcomed his lower-class guests with genuine friendliness, rather than showing off with extravagant food; as a lawyer, he undertook the defense of clients whom everyone else declined, always showing up to court well prepared; he enjoyed mingling with humble and obscure individuals, greeting them by name and chatting for some time. Thanks to these qualities, which were unusual among first-century BCE Roman nobles, Crassus acquired a good deal of popularity. Moreover, he lent out money to friends without interest, but he was so unyielding with deadlines that most borrowers would rather pay interest than rely on Crassus.

This strictness led to the vice that ancient writers ascribe to Crassus: greed. In a biography (from which selections 3 and 4 are taken), Plutarch went as far as affirming that this one vice obfuscated Crassus's many good qualities. Plutarch wrote in Greek, and ancient Greek has more than one word broadly corresponding to English "greed" and "avarice." Plutarch used *philoploutía,* or "love of wealth." The first part of the biography tells the story of how philoploutía led Crassus to accumulate 7,100 talents starting from less than 300 (which, to be sure, was already a considerable sum). The second part elucidates how philoploutía made him lose it all.

Still in his twenties, Crassus seized a first opportunity to feed his greed by serving as a lieutenant under the dictator Sulla. In the late 80s BCE, Sulla ended a bloody civil war by executing his opponents and by confiscating their property. Executions and confiscations were carried out with Roman efficiency. Once someone had been identified as an opponent, he would be "proscribed," meaning that his name was "written up front" in a public list. Proscribed people were wanted, and whoever captured one of them would keep a big share of the victim's confiscated possessions. The rest of the property was sold cheaply but not easily, because most Romans had at least some scruples. Crassus, however, had no such scruples, and selection 3 explains how his fortune took off thanks to proscriptions and other calamities.

In 55 BCE, Crassus and Pompey were consuls and therefore the most powerful men in Rome. Like Crassus, Pompey had served under Sulla, meaning that the same master had taught both the art of ruling forcefully. Indeed, on more than one occasion, the "Sullan" consuls recurred to violence. They reached their goals but met much resistance, and their popularity sank. As seen in selection 1, Pompey failed to regain popular approval by offering lavish entertainment in the same year. By the end of his consulship, Crassus's stocks had plummeted as well, and he must have felt ready to leave Rome for a while. He decided to continue his political career serving as a provincial governor. When the lots for provincial assignments were cast, Crassus drew Syria.

Crassus entered Syria determined to wage war against the Parthians. He invested heavily in the campaign and allegedly even built an entire army at his own expense. He estimated that conquering the wealthy kingdom of Parthia (broadly corresponding to modern Iran) would abundantly repay his investment. But his greed impeded his strategy. Crassus wasted precious time counting the income collected from tributary cities. This unconcealed concern with money lost him the provincials' loyalty and the soldiers' respect (see selection 4). In 53 BCE he fought the Parthians near Carrhae (in the southeast corner of modern Turkey and only a dozen miles from the border with modern Syria). In a disastrous battle, Crassus lost his younger son, Publius, who had served under Caesar in Gaul, and who died an honorable but miserable death. Having witnessed the destruction of most of his army along with that of his son, Crassus accepted a parley, which concealed an ambush. Crassus was slain, and, according to an ancient tradition, the Parthians poured molten gold into his mouth to mock his greed.

Ὅτε γὰρ Σύλλας ἑλὼν τὴν πόλιν ἐπώλει τὰς οὐσίας τῶν ἀνηρημένων ὑπ᾽ αὐτοῦ, λάφυρα καὶ νομίζων καὶ ὀνομάζων, καὶ βουλόμενος ὅτι πλείστοις καὶ κρατίστοις προσομόρξασθαι τὸ ἄγος, οὔτε λαμβάνων οὔτ᾽ ὠνούμενος ἀπεῖπε.

πρὸς δὲ τούτοις ὁρῶν τὰς συγγενεῖς καὶ συνοίκους τῆς Ῥώμης κῆρας ἐμπρησμοὺς καὶ συνιζήσεις διὰ βάρος καὶ πλῆθος οἰκοδομημάτων, ἐωνεῖτο δούλους ἀρχιτέκτονας καὶ οἰκοδόμους. εἶτ᾽ ἔχων τούτους ὑπὲρ πεντακοσίους ὄντας, ἐξηγόραζε τὰ καιόμενα καὶ γειτνιῶντα τοῖς καιομένοις, διὰ φόβον καὶ ἀδηλότητα τῶν δεσποτῶν ἀπ᾽ ὀλίγης τιμῆς προϊεμένων, ὥστε τῆς Ῥώμης τὸ πλεῖστον μέρος ὑπ᾽ αὐτῷ γενέσθαι.

τοσούτους δὲ κεκτημένος τεχνίτας οὐδὲν ᾠκοδόμησεν αὐτὸς ἢ τὴν ἰδίαν οἰκίαν, ἀλλ᾽ ἔλεγε τοὺς φιλοικοδόμους αὐτοὺς ὑφ᾽ ἑαυτῶν καταλύεσθαι χωρὶς ἀνταγωνιστῶν. ὄντων δ᾽ αὐτῷ παμπόλλων ἀργυρείων, πολυτιμήτου δὲ χώρας καὶ τῶν ἐργαζομένων ἐν αὐτῇ, ὅμως ἄν τις ἡγήσαιτο μηδὲν εἶναι ταῦτα πάντα πρὸς τὴν τῶν οἰκετῶν τιμήν· τοσούτους ἐκέκτητο καὶ τοιούτους, ἀναγνώστας, ὑπογραφεῖς, ἀργυρογνώμονας, διοικητάς, τραπεζοκόμους, αὐτὸς ἐπιστατῶν μανθάνουσι καὶ προσέχων καὶ διδάσκων καὶ ὅλως νομίζων τῷ δεσπότῃ προσήκειν μάλιστα τὴν περὶ τοὺς οἰκέτας ἐπιμέλειαν ὡς ὄργανα ἔμψυχα τῆς οἰκονομικῆς.

3–4. ASCENT AND DECLINE OF A GREEDY MAN, PLUTARCH, LIFE OF CRASSUS (ΚΡΑΣΣΟΣ) 2 AND 17, EXCERPTS

When Sulla, having taken Rome, was selling off the possessions of those he had proscribed, he called this "war booty." Sulla wished to blame these proscriptions on other powerful men, and Crassus never declined to take and buy the victims' property. Moreover, seeing that fire and collapse due to the weight and proximity of buildings were quite common incidents in Rome, he bought slaves who were architects and builders. Once he had more than five hundred of these slaves, he began to buy buildings that were burning down or close to those burning, since the owners were selling them for very little money because of fear and uncertainty. Thus, the greater part of Rome fell into his hands.

Even though he owned so many builders, he built nothing for himself aside from his private house; in fact, he used to say that those who like constructions bring ruin on themselves, with no need for enemies. He possessed many silver mines, prized land, and people to work it, and yet one may think that all of this was nothing compared to the value of his slaves. He owned many and skilled slaves (including readers, scribes, silver workers, accountants, and waiters); he personally oversaw their education, getting involved with teaching them. He was fully convinced that a

Καὶ τοῦτο μὲν ὀρθῶς ὁ Κράσσος, εἴπερ, ὡς ἔλεγεν, ἡγεῖτο τὰ μὲν ἄλλα διὰ τῶν οἰκετῶν χρῆναι, τοὺς δὲ οἰκέτας δι᾽ αὑτοῦ κυβερνᾶν· τὴν γὰρ οἰκονομικὴν ἐν ἀψύχοις χρηματιστικὴν οὖσαν, ἐν ἀνθρώποις πολιτικὴν γιγνομένην ὁρῶμεν· ἐκεῖνο δὲ οὐκ εὖ, τὸ μηδένα νομί-ζειν μηδὲ φάσκειν εἶναι πλούσιον, ὃς οὐ δύναται τρέ-φειν ἀπὸ τῆς οὐσίας στρατόπεδον (ὁ γὰρ πόλεμος οὐ τεταγμένα σιτεῖται, κατὰ τὸν Ἀρχίδαμον, ὥσθ᾽ ὁ πρὸς πόλεμον πλοῦτος ἀόριστος). . . .

Τοῦτο πρῶτον ἁμαρτεῖν ἔδοξεν ὁ Κράσσος μετά γε τὴν στρατείαν αὐτὴν μέγιστον ἁμάρτημα τῶν γενομένων, ὅτι πρόσω χωρεῖν δέον ἔχεσθαί τε Βαβυλῶνος καὶ Σελευκείας, δυσμενῶν ἀεὶ Πάρθοις πόλεων, χρόνον ἐνέδωκε τοῖς πολεμίοις παρασκευῆς. ἔπειτα τὰς ἐν Συρίᾳ διατριβὰς ᾐτιῶντο χρηματιστικὰς μᾶλλον οὔσας ἢ στρατηγικάς· οὐ γὰρ ὅπλων ἀριθμὸν ἐξετάζων οὐδὲ γυμνασίων ποιούμενος ἁμίλλας, ἀλλὰ προσόδους πόλεων ἐκλογιζόμενος καὶ τὰ χρήματα τῆς ἐν Ἱεραπόλει θεοῦ σταθμοῖς καὶ τρυτάναις μεταχειριζόμενος ἐπὶ πολ-λὰς ἡμέρας, ἐπιγράφων δὲ καὶ δήμοις καὶ δυνάσταις στρατιωτῶν καταλόγους, εἶτ᾽ ἀνιεὶς ἀργύριον διδόντας, ἠδόξει καὶ κατεφρονεῖτο τούτοις.

master's job should mainly be to take care of his slaves—that is, of a household's living tools.

In this respect, Crassus was right. He used to say that everything had to take place through the slaves, but the slaves had to be guided by him. For we see that if one views slaves as tools, running a household is like running a business, but if one views them as people, it becomes like running a state. In another saying, however, he was not right; he thought and said that no one is rich, unless he can afford to feed an army out of pocket. In fact, as Archidamus has it, one cannot feed a predetermined amount to war, meaning that the money for a war cannot be fixed.

The following could be considered the first mistake by Crassus—without counting the expedition itself, which was the greatest mistake of all. He should have marched all the way to Babylon and Seleucia, which have always been enemies to the Parthians, but instead he gave his enemies time to get ready. He was accused of wasting time in Syria worrying about money more than the war. Indeed, he did not count his troops and weapons, and he failed to organize athletic competitions. Instead, he counted the income of cities and spent various days measuring the wealth of the goddess in Hierapolis, dealing with weights and scales. He also filed lists of soldiers to be enlisted from local peoples and monarchs, but if they offered him silver, he gave in. Thus, he was no longer respected and instead was disdained by them.

Texts 5 and 6. Introduction: Investing in War

According to Plutarch, the Parthians reported limited casualties, but twenty thousand Romans who had followed Crassus died on the battlefield, ten thousand more were captured and killed, and only a few survivors escaped. Who were these people? The ancient sources name only a small number of individuals: Gaius Cassius Longinus (one of the best-known conspirators who would murder Caesar in 44) was thirty-three years old; being one of Crassus's high military officers, he gathered some scattered soldiers and managed to return safely; the other eight officers we can name died in the campaign. Supposedly, some had joined the expedition in order to launch a military or a political career, as Cassius and Crassus's son did; some others, such as a certain Censorinus, may have already been senators, and hence older and more experienced. We know nothing about all the other soldiers, not even their names. While Crassus was in Syria, Caesar was conquering Gaul, and other generals were engaged on other fronts, with mixed results, falling somewhere between Crassus's spectacular defeat and Caesar's spectacular victories. Caesar lavishly rewarded his legionnaires, squandering the huge wealth he had stolen from thousands of massacred or enslaved "barbarians." From a Roman perspective, his soldiers lucked out, as pointed out by

Catullus, a contemporary poet, who pokes some fun at two friends and at himself. Veranus and Fabullus followed Memmius, and they got duped by enduring much hardship for little reward, just as Catullus, who campaigned under an unnamed leader, did. Catullus's disappointment is further increased by noting that another acquaintance, Mamurra, made a fortune by following Caesar instead.

Pisonis comites, cohors inanis,
aptis sarcinulis et expeditis,
Verani optime tuque mi Fabulle,
quid rerum geritis? Satisne cum isto
vappa frigoraque et famem tulistis?
. . .
At vobis mala multa di deaeque
dent, opprobria Romuli Remique.

Quis hoc potest videre, quis potest pati,
nisi impudicus et vorax et aleo,
Mamurram habere quod Comata Gallia
habebat uncti et ultima Britannia?
Cinaede Romule haec videbis et feres? . . .

5. ENROLLING UNDER THE WRONG GENERAL, CATULLUS, POEM 28, EXCERPTS

Comrades of Piso, useless bunch, with your fitting and light baggage, excellent Veranus and you, my dear Fabullus, how are things? Have you endured enough cold and hunger under that useless commander? . . . May the gods and the goddesses punish you, the shameful [generals,] descendants of Romulus and Remus.

6. ENROLLING UNDER THE RIGHT GENERAL (CAESAR), CATULLUS, POEM 29, EXCERPTS

Who can take this, who can endure—unless one is shameless, insatiable, or a gambler—that Mamurra now possesses the wealth that used to belong to Gaul and to Britain? Shameless Romulus, will you put up with these things under your eyes?

Chapter 6

THE DARK SIDE OF MONEY MAKING

Human Trafficking

Introduction

Various forms of human trafficking, including prostitution, renting out gladiators, and selling slaves, were legal, lucrative, and widespread. In fact, it is hard to overestimate the scale and impact of human trafficking in the Roman Empire. Romans invented gladiators, and even if prostitution and slavery were not exclusively Roman phenomena, they became somewhat essential traits of the Roman world.

Lupa, meaning "she-wolf," was an offensive Latin word for "prostitute," which might be compared to "bitch" in modern English. For this reason, in narrating the legendary foundation of Rome, Livy tells the story of the lupa who nourished Romulus and Remus, after they had been abandoned. Livy specifies that according to the official legend, an actual she-wolf fed the twins. Her care and tenderness might have suggested to some that even wild nature providentially contributed to the survival of Rome's founder.

Moreover, wolf milk might account for Romulus's and Remus's superhuman courage and strength. Sculptures, coins, and other images representing the infant twins suckling from the she-wolf were scattered throughout the Roman Empire, reminding everyone of this foundation myth. Yet one versed in the colloquies of ancient Rome might (and did) justly wonder: were the twins actually found and raised by a prostitute? Livy did not choose between the two versions, but he chose to report both. While Livy was writing his history of Rome, emperor Augustus was restoring the Empire by appealing to its mythical foundations. Augustus must have hated the unofficial version of the legend. Whether he liked it or not, a hard-to-die tradition placed prostitution right at the heart of Rome's origins.

Gladiators were a Roman invention. After the first combat was staged in the forum, which was the very center of Rome, the practice spread and became a defining feature of the Roman Empire. The new show provided the occasion for another Roman invention: the amphitheater, whose primary function was hosting gladiatorial games. The word "amphitheater" means "all-around theater," because it resembles the shape of two Greek or Roman theaters, which were semicircular, lined up face to face. Like modern stadiums, the typical amphitheater had an oval shape with 360-degree raised seating. This structure became a mark of the Empire and can still be admired in roughly

230 samples not only in Italy, but also in other countries, including Tunisia, Morocco, Libya, England, Cyprus, Croatia, Spain, France, Romania, Greece, and Syria.

Slavery was practiced all around the Mediterranean, but the number and percentage of slaves reached an unprecedented height under the Romans. It has been calculated that by the end of the first century BCE, roughly 20 to 30 percent of the population of Italy were slaves. Despite these high numbers, we have no account from a slave telling us what it was like to work as a prostitute or a gladiator, or to be kidnapped and sold on the market in the Roman world. Some comparative data will compensate for this vacuum, with evidence from American history and from contemporary realities—a reminder that, according to the data by UNESCO, in 2021 more than twenty-seven million human beings were forced into slavery.

Slave traders, owners of gladiators, and pimps were deeply despised by Romans. This loathing was partially due to the awareness that traffickers catered to base human desires and made a living by putting another person's body on sale. Roman legal texts commonly call a prostitute someone who *corpore quaestum facit*, which literally means a person who "makes a living by the body." Though referring to prostitutes, the periphrasis could equally apply to those who traffic them. For the same reason, Romans looked down at actors; their occupation was disreputable, because they entertained with their body, as prostitutes and gladiators did. And yet, human trafficking was pervasive and profitable.

Texts 1 and 2. Introduction: Trafficking and Prostitution

In the Roman world, male and female sex was for sale and easily accessible. Prostitutes were mostly enslaved. Evidence suggests that most prostitutes did not choose their profession but were forced by their masters or by a relative, especially by a father or a husband, who had power over them. Extreme poverty could lead women to prostitution as well, but in the great majority of cases, prostitutes remained poor and destitute, while other people reaped the benefit of their work. In this respect, Latin terminology is misleading. *Meretrix*, the most common Latin word for "female prostitute," literally means "a woman who earns" (from *mereo*, which means "to earn," and the suffix *-trix*, which typically indicates a female agent). Paradoxically, English language reveals more about the status of Roman prostitutes than Latin does. "Prostitute" derives from the Latin verb *prostituo*, which literally means "to place/set before"; the verb came to indicate pimps publicly exposing their "merchandise." Specifically, "prostitute" comes from the past particle, *prostituta*, which literally indicates a female being "exposed for sale (by someone else)." Indeed, in the greatest majority of documented cases, women were exposed and exploited, while pimps kept the gains.

Latin often employs *scortum* (plural *scorta*) for "prostitute," and since *scortum* is neuter, it applies to male and female individuals alike. Enslaved scorta were primarily based in brothels and managed by a pimp, who could be either free or enslaved, and either male (with a male pimp being called a *leno*, plural *lenones*) or female (*lena*, plural *lenae*). Whether they owned the scorta or they managed them for someone else, lenones and lenae are regularly portrayed by ancient sources as cruel and greedy. They supervised the workers, providing for their basic needs, and they put them to work, setting the prices and collecting the money. If slaves were allowed to claim some money, they allegedly had to repay it to their master for debts incurred. This exploitation sadly resembles the experience of sex trafficking in our world today. Around the world, traffickers manage to enslave other human beings through debt bondage, when a debt (often fabricated and expandable) is used to force into prostitution defenseless people, such as immigrants and refugees.

Brothels, called *lupanaria* (literally meaning "she-wolf dens"; singular *lupanar*), were common and easily accessible in Rome and in Roman towns, as evidence especially from Pompeii has demonstrated. Small inscriptions with the name of a girl or a boy and a price were set on the top frame of doors, each giving access to a small room, *cella*, where clients were received. Lupanaria were filthy and self-enclosed. Selection 2 implies that just stepping into one of these places would have been enough to debase a girl morally. The people working inside must have felt imprisoned, but they might enjoy some comradery. They shared meals and gossip; they welcomed new colleagues with a kiss and took care of their education by teaching the tricks of the trade. Aside from brothels, Romans could find (male and female) sex for sale in bars and inns, circuses, theaters, amphitheaters, and baths, and around forums and even around temples. Moreover, prostitutes were mobile: they could visit clients or trail after crowds gathered for public festivals and shows or stationed in military camps.

Prices varied, but typically they were low, ranging from around 2 asses to a denarius (2 asses was the cost of a cheap loaf of bread, and starting from 133 BCE, a denarius corresponded to 16 asses). Lenones usually imposed many encounters in order to increase their income. Indeed, studies on modern prostitution have demonstrated that, on average, cheaper streetwalkers tend to make more than more expensive call girls. Typical clients included slaves and lower-class individuals, but lupanaria catered to upper-class men, as well. For example, once Elder Cato, whom we met earlier, noticed a renowned nobleman leaving a prostitute and publicly exclaimed, "Well done!" Cato was not being sarcastic, and his reaction reflects a typical Roman attitude. Going with a prostitute was considered a proper way of avoiding fornication and leaving respectable wives alone. Apparently, before long Cato surprised the same man coming out of the same lupanar, and this time he qualified his compliment, specifying that one thing is to go with a prostitute every once in a while, and another is to make a lupanar your home. Once again, Cato's attitude expresses a quintessentially Roman view. On the one hand, there is nothing wrong with using prostitutes in moderation, but on the other hand, excess in sexual fervor met stern disapproval. Clearly, Romans held a shameless double standard. Females would lose their honor by simply stepping into a brothel, while males who occasionally accessed them might be praised.

Although providing a socially acceptable service, prostitutes and pimps were held in low esteem and marked with *infamia*. *Infamia* was used to label persons of ill repute as morally inferior and penalize them with legal restrictions. For this reason, prostitutes and pimps were barred from marrying free Roman citizens, from becoming Roman priestesses, and from representing other people in court or acting as legal witnesses. In fact, women had limited access to these venues anyway, thus the restrictions deriving from infamia particularly applied to prostituted males and to lenones.

Since it was legal, prostitution could be regulated. The state reaped some taxes both from public buildings rented out for prostitution and from prostitutes' earnings. Hence, the Romans felt the need to define what counts as a prostitute. Selection 1, a passage from the *Digesta*, discusses one such legal definition. For Roman jurists, the most salient defining trait of a prostitute was not the place where one practiced, or the number of relations; it did not even concern the money received for service. The discriminating factor was the absence of free will. For this reason, the line separating free and enslaved prostitutes became invisible; after all, they all lacked freedom. The same infamia branded prostitutes and pimps alike. A few laws granted some protection for prostitutes against greedy pimps: a master selling an enslaved individual could put a restriction forbidding the purchaser to prostitute him or her; starting from the second century CE, slaves could not be sold to pimps without some misbehavior having been proven; and freed individuals were allowed to refuse demeaning services to their former masters.

The second selection includes passages from the *Controversiae* by Elder Seneca (ca. 50 BCE–40 CE). Elder Seneca was father of Younger Seneca, a philosopher and preceptor of Nero who surpassed his father's fame. Elder Seneca's oratorical activity exemplifies the practices of his time. In the Roman Republic, ambitious citizens studied rhetoric to learn how to swing an assembly or win the approval of a panel of judges. With the end of the Republic, however, emperors took control of the major political and judicial decisions, and rhetoric declined. Indeed, rhetoric sunk into virtuoso school exercises or public performances, called declamations. As a type of declamation, *controversiae* consisted in a fictitious debate between opposing sides on some controversial issue. Our *controversia* concerns a girl who, having been kidnapped by pirates and sold to a pimp, became a prostitute. She did not belong in the lupanar, so she begged her clients to leave her chaste, but a soldier refused to and tried to take her. She fought back, killed the soldier, was prosecuted, but was absolved. After returning to her parents, she sought to become a priestess, and the controversia debates whether or not she should she be allowed to enter the priesthood. Some imaginary contenders take sides in favor of or against the girl, and although the case is fictitious, their arguments provide insight into the Roman understanding of freedom, responsibility, and infamia.

Palam quaestum facere dicemus non tantum eam, quae in lupanario se prostituit, verum etiam si qua (ut adsolet) in taberna cauponia vel qua alia pudori suo non parcit.

Palam autem sic accipimus passim, hoc est sine dilectu: non si qua adulteris vel stupratoribus se committit, sed quae vicem prostitutae sustinet. Item quod cum uno et altero pecunia accepta commiscuit, non videtur palam corpore quaestum facere. Octavenus tamen rectissime ait etiam eam, quae sine quaestu palam se prostituerit, debuisse his connumerari. Non solum autem ea quae facit, verum ea quoque quae fecit, etsi facere desiit, lege notatur: neque enim aboletur turpitudo, quae postea intermissa est. Non est ignoscendum ei, quae obtentu paupertatis turpissimam vitam egit.

Lenocinium facere non minus est quam corpore quaestum exercere. Lenas autem eas dicimus, quae mulieres quaestuarias prostituunt. Lenam accipiemus et eam, quae alterius nomine hoc vitae genus exercet. Si qua cauponam exercens in ea corpora quaestuaria habeat (ut multae adsolent sub praetextu instrumenti cauponii prostitutas mulieres habere), dicendum hanc quoque lenae appellatione contineri.

1. A LEGAL DEFINITION, DIGEST OF ROMAN LAWS (DIGESTA) XXIII 2.43.1–9

We declare that a woman openly practices prostitution not only when she has put herself for sale in a brothel, but also if she regularly does so in a tavern or if she has no regard for her dignity in any other place.

By "openly," we mean "without discriminating," that is, "openly" does not apply to a woman who gives herself to adulterers or fornicators, but to one who holds the position of a prostitute. Moreover, a woman sleeping with one or two people for money does not count as an "open" prostitute. Nevertheless, Octavenus most rightly affirms that if a woman openly practices prostitution, even if she does not accept money, she must be counted among them. By law, not only a woman who currently practices prostitution is branded with infamy, but also one who used to be a prostitute, even if she quit; for a disgrace that has been paused does not disappear. A woman who has practiced the most shameful life because of poverty should not be excused.

Procuring prostitutes is no less severe than selling oneself. By "procurers," we indicate women who prostitute other women for profit. But a woman who conducts that kind of life on someone else's account we should equally consider a procurer. If a woman who runs an inn keeps prostitutes as part of it (as many typically conceal prostitutes under the

SACERDOS CASTA E CASTIS, PVRA E PVRIS SIT.

Quaedam virgo a piratis capta venit; empta a lenone et prostituta est. Venientes ad se exorabat stipem. Militem, qui ad se venerat, cum exorare non posset, colluctantem et vim inferentem occidit. Accusata et absoluta remissa ad suos est; petit sacerdotium. . . .

IVNI GALLIONIS. Ambitiosa lex est: ad sacerdotium non ullas (nisi integrae) non sanctitatis tantum sed felicitatis admittit; inquirit in maiores, in corpus, in vitam: vide, quemadmodum tam morosae legi satisfacias. Capta es a piratis: inter sicarios, inter homicidas in illis myoparonis angustiis posita es. Viderimus, quid in te audere potuerit feritas hostium, libido barbarorum, licentia dominorum. Certum habeo, iudices, cum hanc feritatem barbarorum audiatis, favetis illi, ut quam primum mutet servitutem <sacerdotio>. Sic istam servaverunt piratae, quemadmodum qui lenoni essent vendituri. . . . Aliquis fortasse inventus est, quem hoc ipsum inritaret, quod rogabas. Ipse autem leno pepercit? Ignoramus istos, quibus vel hoc in eiusmodi quaestu praecipue placet, quod illibatam virginitatem decerpunt? Servavit te

cover of waitresses), this woman as well must be included in the definition of procurer.

2. A FICTITIOUS DEBATE ON INFAMIA, ELDER SENECA, CONTROVERSIES (CONTROVERSIAE) I 2, EXCERPTS

Let a priestess be chaste and pure and of chaste and pure origins.

A girl was captured by pirates and sold. A pimp bought and prostituted her. She regularly asked for a donation from her clients. She tried to ask a soldier who had come to her, but he fought her, recurring to violence, and she killed him. Having been charged and absolved, she was sent back to her parents, and now she seeks the priesthood. . . .

A case against the girl by Iunius Bassus. The law sets a high bar; it admits to the priesthood no woman unless she has impeccable integrity and also good fortune. It examines her ancestors, her body, her conduct. See if you can meet such a high standard. You have been captured by pirates; you have been placed among assassins and murderers in their crowded ship. We shall see what savage enemies, lustful barbarians, and licentious masters had the chance to do to you. One thing I know, judges: once you hear about the savage barbarians, you'll be well disposed toward her, so she can exchange her enslavement for the priesthood! The pirates protected her because they planned to sell her to a pimp! . . . Perhaps someone

leno, quam prostiturus erat in libidinem populi? Ita est: sic leno tamquam nos: 'castam [tam] e castis'. "Omnes, inquit, exorabam:" si quis dubitabat, an meretrix esset, audiat, quam blanda sit. Haesisti in complexu: osculo pacta es; ut felicissima fueris, pro pudicitia impudice rogasti. Quid faciam mulieri inter crimina sua delitescenti? Cum dico: "vim passa es," "occidi, inquit; cum dico: "hominem occidisti," "inferebat, inquit, vim mihi;" sacerdos nostra stuprum homicidio, homicidium stupro defendit. . . .

ALBVCIVS dixit: nescio quis feri et violenti animi venit, ipsis credo dis illum impellentibus, ut futurae sacerdotis non violaret castitatem (sed) vindicaret. Praedixit illi, abstineret a sacro corpore manum: "non est, quod audeas laedere pudicitiam, quam homines servant, dii expectant." Ridenti et in perniciem ruenti suam "en, inquit, arma, quae nescis te ferre pro pudicitia," et raptum gladium in pectus stupratoris mersit. Hoc factum eius ne lateret, iisdem dis immortalibus fuit curae: accusator inventus est, qui pudicitiae eius in foro testimonium redderet. Nemo credebat occisum virum a femina, iuvenem a puella, armatum ab inermi; maior res videbatur, quam ut posset credi sine deorum immortalium adiutorio gesta.

SILO POMPEIVS hac figura narravit: eam vobis sacerdotem promitto, quam incestam nulla facere possit fortuna. Potest aliquam servitus cogere: servit et barbaris et piratis, inviolata apud illos mansit.

approached her, and her very request to be spared provoked him. And did the pimp himself not touch you? Don't we know those people who especially enjoy one thing in their business: to deflower virgins! A pimp spared you to put your body on sale for other people's pleasure? Really? Just like us, the pimp cared that you remain "chaste and of chaste origins?" "But," she says, "I begged every single client to respect me!" Let the ones who doubted whether she was a prostitute hear how charming she is. You lingered in men's embraces, and with a kiss you agreed to their deal. However successful you were, you had to compromise your chastity even as you begged for it. How should I deal with a woman who conceals herself behind her own crimes? If I say, "you suffered violence," then she replies, "I killed"; if I say, "you killed a man," then she replies, "he was using force against me." This priestess of ours defends her violation with homicide, and homicide with her violation. . . .

A case for the girl by Albucius. A brutal and violent man approached her. I think that the gods themselves drove him not to violate the future priestess's chastity but to promote it. She warned him to keep his hands off her holy body: "you would not dare to violate the chastity that the people respect and the gods expect." As he was laughing and rushing to his own ruin, she told him, "check your weapon, which you hold in support of chastity without realizing it." She

Potest aliquam corrumpere prolapsi in vitia saeculi prava consuetudo et iam matronarum multum in libidine magisterium: pudica permanebit. Licet illam ponatis in lupanari; et per hoc illi intactam pudicitiam efferre contigit. Fuit in loco turpi, probroso, leno illam prostituit: populus adoravit; nemo non plus ad servandam pudicitiam contulit quam quod ad violandam attulerat. Multum potest ad certum quoque pudici animi propositum hostis gladio: non succumbet, immo, si opus fuerit, pudicitiam vindicabit. Incredibilem videor in puella rem promittere; iam praestitit:

snatched his sword and sunk it into his breast. The gods took care that this deed of hers be known. A witness stepped up and testified to her chastity in court. No one believed that a woman killed a man, a girl a young adult, and that he had a weapon, but she did not. It was more than one could believe had happened without the intervention of the immortal gods.

Silo Pompeius used this illustration: I bring before you a priestess, whom no adversity could make unchaste. A woman can be forced into slavery. She was enslaved to barbarians and pirates but remained unviolated even among them. A woman can be corrupted by the bad morals of our degenerate times, as abundantly witnessed by depraved married women, but this woman will stay pure. You may place her in a brothel, and she will walk away chaste even from there. She was in a disgraceful place. A pimp used her as a prostitute, but the people adored her, and to preserve her chastity every single man contributed more money than they would pay to violate it. Great is the power of an enemy who has a sword, even against the fixed resolve of a pure mind. But she will not surrender, and indeed, if it comes down to it, she will avenge her chastity. With this girl I seem to promise something impossible: but she has delivered already. She has rejected a young man with

adulescentem misericordis populi beneficium pollu-
ere temptantem gladio reppulit. Fuit qui illam accu-
saret caedis: absoluta est. Ne qua posset esse vobis
dubitatio, quae ventura ad sacerdotium erat an pura
esset, an integra, iam iudicatum est.

a sword as he tried to pollute the chastity that the merciful Romans recognize. One came forth to accuse her of homicide; she was absolved. So that you may have no doubt, a verdict has already been passed as to whether the one who is becoming a priestess is chaste and innocent.

Texts 3 and 4. Introduction: Trafficking and Gladiators

As seen above, Romans labeled those who "make a living by the body" with infamia. Hence gladiators, prostitutes, and pimps, known as *infames*, were seen as morally inferior and deprived of certain civic rights. In fact, these people shared more than just infamia. Like prostitutes, gladiators could be enslaved or free, but since they all worked and lived under cruel lanistae, this distinction made little difference. Gladiators had to take an oath committing to obey a lanista who supervised their life and training, and who signed contracts to rent them out for shows. Having taken their oaths, gladiators regularly fought against their teammates and friends.

Like prostitutes, gladiators lived in secluded communities, called *ludi* (singular *ludus*), and might enjoy some comradery. They lived and ate together. However, since they were divided in categories depending on skill and rental price, they trained in separate groups. Daily training was directed by one or more coaches, or *magistri*, and consisted of physical exercise, practicing set defensive and offensive moves, or *dictata*, and scrimmage fights with wooden swords. Archaeological remains have shown that gladiators slept in quite small cells, and there is some evidence of complaints about filthy ludi. Archaeology has also revealed that some gladiators were chained at night, but lanistae must have left the rest free to leave a ludus between training sessions. Some gladiators were married and lived with their family, but *familia gladiatoria* does not typically refer to such families. Rather, it indicates the entire team of gladiators belonging to the same ludus, thus this term provides one more indicator of their sense of comradery.

Game sponsors, called *editores* (singular *editor*), paid high prices for renting gladiators, but lanistae kept all the profit they could for themselves. In fact, they found a way to feed the gladiators and spend as little as possible. Gladiators' food was commonly called *sagina*, a Latin noun originally indicating the rich nourishment used for fattening animals. Being cheap and nutritious, barley, *hordeum*, made up such a large part of gladiators' daily sagina, that they were often called *hordearii*, meaning "barley men." Gladiators, however, could save money on the side. If they were enslaved, they could hope either to buy their freedom and then leave the ludus or to sign a contract as free people and continue to conduct the same life. Free gladiators tried to save money as well, and after their contract with the lanista had expired, they could seek another contract or leave the ludus.

Normally gladiators did not fight to the death, but many died before abandoning a ludus. Gladiatorial fights were meant to entertain, and gladiators knew that their combats had to please the spectators. Younger Seneca disapprovingly reports some comments commonly heard in amphitheaters: "Kill him!" "Burn him alive!" "Why is that one so timid in facing the opponent's sword?" "Force that one with wounds to risk being wounded!" "Don't protect your chest as you exchange blows!" As seen in chapter 4, once a gladiator surrendered, the editor who sponsored the games had the power to have him spared or dispatched. The people pressed the editor shouting *missus!* ("let him go!") or *iugula!* ("cut his throat open!"). This was the moment for which editores had paid the big bucks, with thousands of pairs of eyes fixed on them. If the people were disappointed at a weak fight, they would more likely shout *iugula*, and editores must have felt torn. On the one hand, they could please the masses and second their desire; on the other hand, voting for death would cost up to fifty times as much, as it amounted to buying rather than just renting a gladiator (see selection 3). As a rule, editores who pleased the people were considered good, but bad emperors did not always listen to them. In either case, gladiators just waited for a verdict. Typically, a fight lasted fifteen to twenty minutes, and if a duel protracted for much longer without a clear outcome, a referee could proclaim a draw, but draws occurred rarely.

Gladiatorial games and contracts were regulated by laws. Text 3 is a selection from the writings of Gaius, a Roman jurist, who discussed the legal nature of contracts for gladiators. Selection 4 reproduces an abstract from the minutes of a senatorial discussion regarding gladiatorial shows. Around 177 CE, the senate ratified a recommendation by emperor Marcus Aurelius and passed a law. The law was meant to curb abuses by greedy lanistae, who drained the resources of towns and private sponsors but offered increasingly unimpressive spectacles. But the show must go on. Scholars have observed a direct connection between this law and the sudden (re)eruption of persecutions of Christians. As "criminals," they were cheaper than gladiators, but public executions still entertained the masses. In 177, ten people abjured and forty-eight were martyred in Lyon, France. Free and enslaved men and women alike were killed by wild beasts, by gladiators, and by torture.

The selection below reproduces an intervention by a senator who spoke after emperor Marcus Aurelius and supported his recommendation. This recommendation, which became law, fixed a maximum price for lending out gladiators, depending on their category. From then on, lanistae could no longer charge as they wished. Second, it limited the total amount editores could spend on spectacles offered for profit. Free spectacles had no maximum cost, but lanistae had to provide gladiators belonging to different categories. From then on, lanistae could no longer rent out unexperienced and unknown gladiators only. Finally, the law established the percentage on gains that lanistae had to pay to gladiators. Since local games could be sponsored both by towns, who used tax money, and by imperial magistrates, who used private money, the senator suggested that maximum costs be established depending on public and private resources. To prevent abuses by lanistae and to avoid excessive expenses by editores, imperial authorities would establish maximum costs of games locally and oversee the distribution of gladiators in the set categories.

Item si gladiatores ea lege tibi tradiderim, ut in singulos, qui integri exierint, pro sudore denarii XX mihi darentur, in eos uero singulos, qui occisi aut debilitati fuerint, denarii mille, quaeritur, utrum emptio et uenditio an locatio et conductio contrahatur. Et magis placuit eorum, qui integri exierint, locationem et conductionem contractam uideri, at eorum, qui occisi aut debilitati sunt, emptionem et uenditionem esse; idque ex accidentibus apparet, tamquam sub condicione facta cuiusque uenditione aut locatione. Iam enim non dubitatur, quin sub condicione res uenire aut locari possint.

Senatus consultum de sumptibus ludorum gladiatoriorum minuendis.

... Censeo igitur in primis agendas maximis impp(eratoribus) gratias, qui salutaribus remedis, fisci ratione post habita, labentem civitatium

3. A LEGAL OPINION ON GLADIATORIAL CONTRACTS, GAIUS, INSTITUTIONS OF ROMAN LAW (INSTITUTIONES) III 146

Similarly, imagine that I give gladiators to you with the agreement that you owe me 20 denarii per gladiator who fights and survives combat uninjured, but you owe me 1,000 for each who was killed or disabled. The question is whether this is a purchase or a rental contract. The most common opinion is that for those gladiators who leave uninjured, the contract seems one of rental, but for those who were killed or disabled, it is a contract of purchase. This clearly depends on the outcome; depending on the outcome, each gladiator's contract was stipulated for sale or for rental. For no one any longer doubts that something can be sold or rented conditionally.

4. REGULATIONS LIMITING ENTERTAINMENT EXPENSES, CORPUS OF LATIN INSCRIPTIONS (CORPUS INSCRIPTIONUM LATINARUM) II 6278[1] = SELECTED LATIN INSCRIPTIONS (INSCRIPTIONES LATINAE SELECTAE) 5163, EXCERPTS

Senatorial deliberation regarding the reduction of expenses for gladiatorial games.

. . . Therefore, I believe that we must first of all give thanks to our excellent emperors, because they advanced healthy remedies and did not put the interest

STATUM ET PRAECIPITANTES IAM IN RUINAS PRINCIPA-
LIUM VIRORUM FORTUNA\<S\> RESTITUERUNT, TANTO
QUIDEM MAGNIFICENTIUS, QUOD, CUM EXCUSATUM ESSET
RETINERENT QUAE ALI INSTITUISSENT ET QUAE LONGA
CONSUETUDO CONFIRMASSET, TAMEN ILLI PERAEQUE
NEQUAQUAM SECTAE SUAE CONGRUERE ARBITRATI SUNT
MALE INSTITUTA SERVARE ... *VACAT*

QUAMQUAM AUTEM NON NULLI ARBITRENTUR DE
OMNIBUS QUAE AD NOS MAXIMI PRINCIPES RETTUL-
ERUNT UNA ET SUCCINCTA SENTENTIA CENSENDUM,
TAMEN, SI VOS PROBATIS, SINGULA SPECIALITER PERSE-
QUAR, VERBIS IPSIS EX ORATIONE SANCTISSIMA AD
LUCEM SENTENTIAE TRANSLATIS, NE QUA EX PARTE
PRAVIS INTERPRETATIONIBUS SIT LOCUS. ... ITAQUE
CENSEO UTI MUNERA QUAE ASSIFORANA APPELLAN-
TUR IN SUA FORMA MANEANT NEC EGREDIANTUR
SUMPTU HS **XXX**. QUI AUTEM SUPRA UHS **XXXI** (*SIC*)
AD **LX** USQUE MUNUS EDENT, IS GLADIATORES TRIP-
ERTITO PRAEBEANTUR NUMERO PARI. SUMMUM PRE-
TIUM SIT PRIMAE PARTI QUINQUE MILIA, SECUNDAE
QUATTUOR MILIA, TERTIAE TRIA MILIA.

A HS **LX** AD **C** USQUE TRIFARIAM COETUS
GLADIATOR(UM) DIVISUS SIT: PRIMI ORDINIS GLADIA-
TORIS SUMMUM PRETIUM SIT **VIII**, MEDIAE CLASSIS **VI**,
DEINDE QUINQUE. PORRO A CENTUM MILIBUS AD **CL**
QUINQUE SINT MANIPULI, CUIUS PRIMI PRETIUM SIT
XII, V SECUNDI **X**, TERTI **VIII**, QUARTI **VI**, POSTREMO
QUINQUE. IAM HINC PORRO A **CL** AD **CC** ET QUIDQUID

of the treasury first. They restored both the status of declining townships and the fortunes of the leading men of those towns that were falling into ruin. And it is all the more splendid that they could have kept with impunity what others had initiated and custom had normalized, and yet together they decided that keeping poorly established practices was by no means fitting for their approach . . . [some words are missing].

But even though some people think that we should reach a decision regarding everything our emperors have announced in a single short recommendation, if you do not mind, I plan to discuss it section by section and to cite and explain the exact words from that most illuminated speech [which had just been delivered to the senate by Emperor Marcus Aurelius], lest room be left for base interpretations of any sections.

Accordingly, I move that "the games offered for profit stay as they are and do not exceed the cost of 30,000 sestertii. But those who spend between 30,000 and 60,000 sestertii for gladiatorial combats should display gladiators in equal number in three categories: 5,000 sestertii shall be the maximum cost [per gladiator in] the first category, 4,000 for the second, and 3,000 for the third.

"When it costs between 60,000 and 100,000, the gladiators shall be divided into three categories. The maximum cost per gladiator in the first category shall be 8,000 sestertii; for the second, 6,000; and for the third, 5,000. Then, when the show costs between

SUPRA SUSUM VERS(UM) ERIT, INFIMI GLADIATORIS PRETIUM SIT **VI**, V SUPER EUM **VII**, TERTI RETRO **VIIII**, QUARTI **XII** ADUSQUE **XV** ET HAEC SIT SUMMO AC POSTREMO GLADIATORI DEFINITA QUANTITAS. UTIQUE IN OMNIBUS MUNERIBUS, QUAE GENERATIM DISTINCTA SUNT, LANISTA DIMIDIAM COPIAM UNIVERSI NUMERI PROMISQUAE MULTITUDINIS PRAEBEAT EXQUE HIS, QUI GREGARI APPELLANTUR, QUI MELIOR INTER TALES ERIT DUOBUS MILI[BU]S SUB SIGNO PUGNET, NEC QUISQUAM EX EO NUMERO MILLE NUMMUM MINORE.

LANISTAS ETIAM PROMONENDOS VILI STUDIO QUAESTUS NEC EAM SIBI COPIAM DIMIDIAE PARTIS PRAEBENDAE ESSE EX NUMERO GREGARIORUM, UTI SCIANT INPOSITAM SIBI NECESSITATEM DE CETERIS QUOS MELIORES OPINABUNTUR TRANSFERRE TANTISPER PLENDI NUMERI GREGARIORUM GRATIA. ITAQUE IS NUMERUS UNIVERSAE FAMILIAE AEQUIS PAR[T]IBUS IN SINGULOS DIES DISPARTIATUR, ATQUE NULLO DIE MINUS QUAM DIMIDIA PARS GREGARIORUM SIT IBI QUI EO DIE DIMICABUNT. UTQUE EA OPSERVATIO A LANISTIS QUAM DILIGENTISSIME EXIGATUR, INIUNGENDUM HIS QUI PROVINCIAE PRAESIDEBUNT ET LEGATIS VEL QUAESTORIBUS VEL LEGATIS LEGIONUM VEL IIS QUI IUS DICUNT C(LARISSIMIS) V(IRIS), AUT PROCURATORIBUS MAXIMORUM PRINCIPUM QUIBUS PROVINCIAE RECTOR MANDAVERIT, IS ETIAM PROCURATOR(IBUS) QUI PROVINCIIS PRAESIDEBUNT. . . .

ITEM CENSEO DE EXCEPTIS ITA OPSERVANDUM UT PRAECIPUUM MERCEDIS GLADIATOR SIBI QUISQUE

100,000 and 150,000 sestertii, the gladiators shall be divided into five groups. The maximum cost per gladiator in the first group shall be 12,000 sestertii; for the second, 10,000; for the third, 8,000; for the fourth, 6,000; and for the last, 5,000. Finally, [for those games costing] between 150,000 and 200,000 and up, the maximum cost per gladiator in the lowest category shall be 6,000 sestertii; for the category above, 7,000; for the third, 8,000; for the second, 12,000; and for the first, 15,000. This shall be the maximum amount fixed for a gladiator in the top category."

I also move that in all gladiatorial shows that are subdivided by category, the lanista should exhibit half of the total gladiators who fight in teams; and that among those who are called herd gladiators (*gregarii*), the best among them shall fight under a war banner for 2,000 sestertii maximum; and that no one from the same group shall fight for less than 1,000.

They affirm that lanistae must be warned against seeking base gains, and that they do not have the freedom to exhibit the half from the group of the herd gladiators. They must realize that they have been ordered by law to transfer some of their best gladiators to replenish the category of herd gladiators for a little while. So, from day to day, the total number of gladiators shall be divided in two groups, and the herd gladiators should never be fewer than half of those who fight on a given day. To be sure that the lanistae enact this duty diligently, we must give oversight to

PACISCATUR EIUS PECUNIAE QUAE OB HANC CAUSAM
EXCIPIEBATUR QUARTAM PORTIONEM LIBER, SERVUS
AUTEM QUINTAM ACCIPIAT. DE PRETIS AUTEM GLADI-
ATORUM OPSERVARI PAULO ANTE CENSUI SECUNDUM
PRAESCRIPTUM DIVINAE ORATIONIS, SED UT EA PRETIA
AD EAS CIVITATES PERTINEANT IN QUIBUS AMPLIORA
GLADIATORUM PRETIA FLAGRABANT.

QUOD SI QUIBUS CIVITATIBUS RES PUBLICA TENUIOR
EST, NON EADEM SERVENTUR QUAE AP(UT) FORTIORES
CIVITATES SCRIPTA SUNT; NEC SUPRA MODUM VIRIUM
ONERENT, SED HACTENUS IN EUNDEM; UT QUAE IN PUB-
LICIS PRIVATISQUE RATIONIB[U]S REPPERIENTUR PRE-
TIA SUMMA AC MEDIA AC POSTREMA, SI Q[UI]DEM
PROVINCIARUM EAE CIVITATES SUNT, AB EO QUI PRAE-
SIDEBIT PROVINCIAE OPSERVENTUR. . . .

ATQUE ITA RATI[O]NIBUS DECEM RETROVERSUM AN-
NORUM INSPECTIS, EXEMPLIS MUNERUM IN QUAQUE
CIVITATE EDITORES ERUNT CONSIDERATIS, CONSTI[TUA]
NTUR AB EO CUIUS ARBITRATUS ERIT DE TRIBUS PRE-
TIS; VEL, SI MELIUS EI VIDEBITUR, EX EO MODO
QUEM PERAEQU[E] FI[ER]I LICEBIT TRIFARIAM PRETIA

governors or lieutenants of provinces, military officials, and questors or distinguished judges, or to imperial procurators appointed by provincial authority,
and to the other authorities in charge of provinces
as well. . . .

Likewise, regarding the rewards, I second that we
must make sure that each gladiator shall earn, as his
own pay, a part of the money gained in a given combat. Free gladiators shall receive a quarter, and slave
gladiators a fifth. As for the price of gladiators, I expressed my opinion recently in accordance with the
divine regulation. I only add that the maximum prices
should apply to those towns where expenses for gladiators have gone through the roof.

And if the revenues are thin in certain towns, let us
not apply those laws that were written for wealthier
towns. Let these towns not be excessively burdened,
rather only to the extent that each can support. In this
way, prices turn out to be the highest, medium, and
lowest, both in public and in private accounts, and for
towns in provinces, the maximum price shall be supervised by whomever is in charge of that province. . . .

So, let us inspect the accounts from the last ten
years and take into consideration the previous games
in towns with private sponsors. Then let whoever is
in charge decide the highest, medium, and lowest price,
or if it seems more fitting, he shall determine the price
of each of the three levels in whichever way it allows
him to be just. And let us maintain this approach for

DIDUCANTUR; EAQUE FORMA ETIAM IN POSTERUM
SERVETUR; SCIANTQUE V(IRI) C(LARISSIMI) QUI PRO-
CONSULES PAULO ANTE PROFECTI SUNT INTRA SUUM
QUISQUE ANNUM ID NEGOTIUM EXSEQUI SE OPORTERE,
ET II ETIAM QUI NON SORTITO PROVINCIAS REGUNT [I]
NTRA ANNUM.

the future. The most distinguished men who have already departed from Rome to act as provincial proconsuls shall be informed that each of them has to put these orders into effect within his year in power, and that the same one-year rule applies to those who govern a province they have not received by lot.

Texts 5, 6, and 7. Introduction: Slave Trafficking

Toward the middle of the second century BCE, the small island of Delos (roughly 1.2 square miles) became the center of a complex network in the eastern Mediterranean. On the one hand, Delos lays halfway between Greece and Turkey, and on the other hand, unlike other and bigger islands that have the same strategic position, Delos enjoyed a special status. In 167 BCE, the Romans made it a free port. As a free port, Delos drew in such great numbers of pirates, kidnappers, and slave dealers that it soon became the most important market for slave trade. Archaeological evidence reveals that, as a result, the docks of Delos's main harbor were renovated and enlarged, the population grew, and new and bigger houses were built. The economy flourished, thanks especially to slave trade. The ancient geographer Strabo (ca. 64 BCE–24 CE) writes that "tens of thousands of slaves could be received and dispatched on the same day, so that there was a saying: 'Trader dock here and unload! Your cargo's already been sold.'"[11]

The cargo consisted mainly of victims of war and piracy. As Rome expanded its borders, more and more people were conquered, and some of those became enslaved. A victorious general enjoyed a good amount of discretion: he could grant freedom to his defeated, or slaughter, or enslave them. As a rule, the harder the enemy resistance, the harsher the Roman treatment. Slave traders traveled with Roman armies, ready to prey on war booty. They possessed the staff and the infrastructure to transport thousands of people and then sell them on retail, for large profits. Slave traders and retail dealers met at places like Delos. Once the prisoners reached the market, families and relations could be broken, most of them never to see each other again.

Slave markets consisted of wide areas enclosed between walls or porticoes. Each slave for sale stood on a platform, called *catasta*. They would be semi-naked, so that customers could conduct an inspection. Dealers prepared slaves carefully to make an impression. In his *Natural History*, Elder Pliny gives recommendations for improving their presentation: terebinth resin works miracles for curing the skin of thin slaves, and a woman called Salpe devised a mix of liver and cedar oil for depilating young boys and making them look younger. A small tablet hanging over a slave's neck provided relevant information. Buyers could always ask for more details, and dealers might stop shouting out their sales lines to respond. Slaves on sale could be even asked to demonstrate their health by running a lap. Since some enslaved individuals might be recalcitrant, a law ordered sellers to specify which slaves were war prisoners. Chalked feet and a crown mockingly singled out fresh captives.

No direct account by a Roman slave survives, but among others, there does survive the description of a comparable situation by Olaudah Equiano (ca. 1745–97), who was enslaved and sold at market centuries later. "We were not many days in the merchants' custody before we were sold in the usual manner, which is this: on a signal given, such as the beat of a drum, the buyers rush at once into the yard where the slaves are confined and make choice of that parcel they like the best. The noise and clamor with which this is attended, and the eagerness visible in the countenance of the buyers, serve no little to increase the apprehension of the terrified Africans. . . . In this manner, without scruple, are relations and friends separated, most of them never to see each other again. I remember in the vessel in which I was brought over, in the man's apartment, there were several brothers, who, in the sale, were sold in different lots; and it was very moving on this occasion to see and hear their cries at parting."[12]

Since war provided only an irregular and unreliable flow of slaves, piracy increased to meet the demand. In fact, in spite of being illegal, piracy was so organized and successful that it eventually became the main means of supplementing slaves. Anyone traveling by sea or living on the coast could become a victim of pirates. As a result, the line separating pirates from slave dealers could be blurry, and Romans disliked dealers as much as they did lenones and lanistae. For example, according to Pausanias (second century CE), a group of Illyrian sailors arrived at Mothon, a small town on the southwestern coast of Greece. They bought wine and sold merchandise at cheap prices. Local men and women grew more and more confident, but once they gathered around the ships, the sailors seized so many of them that the town was left deserted. People living on the borders of the Empire could be easily kidnapped and enslaved as well. For example, commerce flourished in the region north of the Sea of Azov, where modern Ukraine borders with Russia. Nomadic tribes from Asia traded slaves in exchange for fabrics and wine. The same happened in North Africa, as exemplified by selection 7.

Once again, we have no direct account from any of those who were kidnapped in ancient Rome, but a more recent account, by Francis Bok in *Escape from Slavery*, can help us to imagine what must have happened at Mothon and in many other parts of the Empire. In 1986, Francis, who was then seven years old, went with some other kids from his village in South Sudan to a market and began selling hard-cooked eggs and peanuts.

> Then something changed. . . . Suddenly everyone was running in every direction. "The murahaliin are coming!" And wherever the people scattered, they ran into men . . . shooting and hacking people to the ground with their swords. . . . "Run!" yelled Nyabol.

"Leave your things and run!" I raced from the marketplace—and right into a huge horse with a militiaman . . . Someone grabbed me from behind. . . . Everyone was crying and screaming for their parents. I was crying, too. What was happening to us? The older kids, including my friends Kwol, Nyabol, and Abuk, were herded into another group and the women into a third. They were all crying.[13]

After being kidnapped, Frances was sold, and he lived as a slave for ten years, until he managed to escape.

In the Roman world, breeding people into slavery provided one more means to meet the demand. Home-born slaves, called *vernae*, could be desirable for more than one reason. By training them to master a skill, their owners could extract more value from them; home-born slaves were spared at least the trauma of being captured and sold; and buyers did not need to rely on the information provided by dealers. Maintaining vernae, however, added to a master's expenses as well. For this reason, Elder Cato pedantically details the necessary and sufficient amount of wine, food, and clothes that a master should allot to slaves (see selection 5). In some cases, Cato's numbers do not completely add up, but one cannot miss the point. Cato clearly wants to keep enslaved people productive with as little as he can. In selection 6, Columella shares some tips about ways to treat slaves. Columella might seem kinder than Cato, but there is no doubt that both were driven by the same desire to maximize slave productivity. For the same reason, Columella recommends rewarding female fertility.

The last selection details the illegal activities of pirates and brigands acting as slave dealers. Throughout North Africa, throngs of criminals roamed in military fashion terrorizing and killing men and enslaving women and youth. At the beginning of the fifth century CE, their raids became so frequent and dangerous that Augustine wrote a letter to his dear friend Alypius. In the last excerpt, Augustine explains what he learned from a young girl who had been kidnapped out of her parents' house. This young girl (probably even younger than Francis Bok) was rescued before reaching the market, but many others were less fortunate.

Familiae cibaria. Qui opus facient: per hiemem tritici modios IIII, per aestatem modios IIII S; vilico, vilicae, epistatae, opilioni: modios III; compeditis: per hiemem panis p. IIII, ubi vineam fodere coeperint panis p. V, usque adeo dum ficos esse coeperint; deinde ad p. IIII redito. Vinum familiae. Ubi vindemia facta erit, loram bibant menses tres; mense quarto heminas in dies, id est in mense congios II S: mense quinto, sexto, septimo, octavo in dies sextarios, id est in mense congios quinque; nono, decimo, undecimo, duodecimo in dies heminas ternas, id est in mense amphoram; hoc amplius Saturnalibus et Conpitalibus in singulos homines congios III S; summa vini in homines singulos inter annum Q. VII. Conpeditis, uti quidquid operis facient, pro portione addito; eos non est nimium in annos singulos vini Q. X ebibere.

Pulmentarium familiae. Oleae caducae quam plurimum condito; postea oleas tempestivas, unde minimum olei fieri poterit, eas condito: parcito uti quam diutissime durent. Ubi oleae comesae erunt, hallacem et acetum dato. Oleum dato in menses unicuique s. I; salis unicuique in anno modium satis est.

5. ASSESSING THE COSTS OF MAINTAINING SLAVES, ELDER CATO, ON AGRICULTURE (DE AGRICULTURA) 56, 58–59

Amount of food for slaves. For manual laborers, four pecks of wheat in winter and four and a half in summer; for the superintendent, his wife, the foreman, and the shepherd, three pecks; for those who work in chains, four pounds of bread in winter, five from when they begin to dig for the vines until the time when the figs ripen, then back to four. Amount of wine for slaves. For three months after the vintage, let them drink the thin wine made of grape husks; on the fourth month, a half pint per day for a total of two and a half congii per month; from the fifth to the eighth month, a pint per day, for a total of five congii; from the ninth to the twelfth month, a pint and half per day, for a total of one amphora per month. On top of this, during the feasts of the Saturnalia and of the Compitalia give each three and a half congii. The total allotment of wine per person is seven amphorae per year. For those who work in chains, increase this amount depending on how much they work. Ten amphorae of wine per person is not too much to drink per year.

Amount of spread for slaves. Store as many fallen olives as you can, then store the ripe olives, which produce little oil. Keep them, so that they can last as long as possible. When you are out of olives, give the slaves

Vestimenta familiae. Tunicam p. III S, saga alternis annis. Quotiens cuique tunicam aut sagum dabis, prius veterem accipito, unde centones fiant. Sculponias bonas alternis annis dare oportet.

In ceteris servis haec fere praecepta servanda sunt, quae me custodisse non paenitet, ut rusticos, qui modo non incommode se gessissent, saepius quam urbanos familiarius adloquerer, et cum hac comitate domini levari perpetuum laborem eorum intellegerem, nonnumquam etiam iocarer et plus ipsis iocari permitterem. Iam illud saepe facio, ut quasi cum peritioribus de aliquibus operibus novis deliberem et per hoc cognoscam cuiusque ingenium, quale quamque sit prudens.

Tum etiam libentius eos id opus adgredi video, de quo secum deliberatum et consilio ipsorum susceptum putant. Nam illa sollemnia sunt omnibus circumspectis, ut ergastuli mancipia recognoscant, ut explorent an diligenter vincti sint, an ipsae sedes custodiae satis tutae

fish sauce and vinegar. Give each a pint of oil per month. As for salt, a couple of gallons per person is enough for a year.

Clothing for slaves. Give them a three-and-a-half foot tunic and a mantle made of rough wool every other year. Before giving any slave a new tunic or mantle, take the old one back, so you can patch it up. You should give each a pair of good clogs every other year.

6. HOW TO MAXIMIZE SLAVE PRODUCTIVITY, COLUMELLA, ON AGRARIAN MATTERS (DE RE RUSTICA) I 8.1–19

Here are the principles that must be generally observed regarding the other slaves. I do not regret that I have personally followed these rules. If country slaves have not behaved improperly, address them with great friendliness more often than the town slaves, and if I felt that my kindness eased their long labor, at times I used jokes as well and even allowed them to do the same. I often do something else. When I have to make a decision about some new job, I consult them as experts, and in this way, I assess their intelligence and wisdom.

As a result, I see them become more eager to do a job for which they feel their input was solicited and taken into account. Moreover, all men of good judgment take care to double-check the slaves' prison, to ascertain whether they are tied properly and whether

munitaeque sint, num vilicus aut alligaverit quempiam domino nesciente aut revinxerit.

Nam utrumque maxime servare debet, ut et quem pater familiae tali poena multaverit, vilicus nisi eiusdem permissu compedibus non eximat et quem ipse sua sponte vinxerit, antequam sciat dominus, non resolvat; tantoque curiosior inquisitio patris familiae debet esse pro tali genere servorum, ne aut in vestiariis aut in ceteris praebitis iniuriose tractentur, quanto et pluribus subiecti, ut vilicis, ut operum magistris, ut ergastulariis, magis obnoxii perpetiendis iniuriis, et rursus saevitia atque avaritia laesi magis timendi sunt. Itaque diligens dominus cum et ab ipsis tum et ab solutis, quibus maior est fides, quaerit, an ex sua constitutione iusta percipiant, atque ipse panis potionisque probitatem gustu suo explorat, vestem, manicas pedumque tegumina recognoscit.

Saepe etiam querendi potestatem faciat de iis, qui aut crudeliter eos aut fraudulenter infestent. Nos quidem aliquando iuste dolentes tam vindicamus, quam animadvertimus in eos, qui seditionibus familiam concitant, qui calumniantur magistros suos; ac rursus praemio prosequimur eos, qui strenue atque industrie se gerunt.

Feminis quoque fecundioribus, quarum in subole certus numerus honorari debet, otium, nonnumquam et libertatem dedimus, cum complures natos educassent. Nam cui tres erant filii, vacatio, cui plures, libertas quoque contingebat.

the very locations of custody are safe and secure enough, and whether the supervisor has bound or unbound a slave without informing the master.

For one must truly beware both that a supervisor does not, without the master's permission, release from shackles a slave condemned to that punishment by the master of the house, and that a supervisor does not free a slave he himself condemned before the master knows about it. And a master of the house's examination of slaves of this kind has to be particularly thorough, so that they are not treated unjustly in the allocation of clothes or other supplies. By being under so many people, such as supervisors, team leaders, and guards, they are exposed to suffering unfairly, and in return for cruelty and greed they become more frightening. Therefore, a diligent master makes an inquiry both from those who are in prison and from those are not (and slaves out of prison are more trustworthy). He asks whether they are treated justly under his charge, he personally tastes the quality of their food and drink, and he checks their clothes, the length of their sleeves, and what they wear on their feet.

He often gives them freedom to complain about whoever treats them with cruelty or treachery. Indeed, sometimes I defend those who have a right to complain, but at the same time I punish those who stir up slaves to revolt or those who speak against their masters for no good reason. To the same end, I reward those who act promptly and diligently.

Addo autem et aliud: tanta est eorum qui uulgo mangones uocantur in Africa multitudo, ut eam ex magna
parte humano genere exhauriant, transferendo quos
mercantur in prouincias transmarinas et paene omnes
liberos. Nam uix pauci reperiuntur a parentibus uenditi,
quos tamen non—ut leges Romanae sinunt—operas
uiginti quinque annorum emunt isti, sed prorsus sic
emunt ut seruos, et uendunt trans mare ut seruos;
ueros autem seruos a dominis omnino rarissime. Porro
ex hac multitudine mercatorum ita insoleuit seducen-
tium et depraedantium multitudo, ita ut gregatim ulu-
lantes habitu terribili uel militari uel barbaro agrestia
quaedam loca, in quibus pauci sunt homines, perhi-
beantur inuadere et quos istis mercatoribus uendant
uiolenter abducere.

Omitto quod nuperrime nobis fama nuntiauerat in
quadam uillula per huiusmodi aggressiones occisis
uiris feminas et pueros ut uenderentur abreptos; sed

There are number of women who are particularly fertile, and they have to be recognized for their offspring. I give them free time and sometimes even freedom, because they raised many children. Specifically, a slave mother of three gets exemption from work, and a mother of more gets her freedom as well.

7. PIRATES AND SLAVE DEALERS, AUGUSTINE, LETTERS (EPISTULAE) 10, EXCERPTS

But there is something else. In Africa, the number of slave traffickers, called *mangones*, is so high that they are draining Africa of much of its human resources. They trade people for profit across the sea, and almost all those people used to be free. Indeed, very few have been sold by their parents, and the traffickers do not rent them for twenty-five years of labor, as allowed by law, but they buy them as though they were slaves, and as slaves they sell them across the sea. In fact, they sell actual slaves sold by a master only very rarely. In turn, a throng of snatchers and pillagers was born out of this mass of dealers, and they have become so daring that I hear they wander in groups with terrifying cries, like soldiers or barbarians. They attack some locations in the countryside where there are few inhabitants and use violence to take people and sell them to the dealers.

I pass over some most recent rumors. In a small country house, they made one of these attacks; the men were killed, and the females and boys were captured to be sold. But I was not told where this

ubi hoc contigerit—si tamen uere contigit—non dice-
batur. Verum ego ipse cum inter illos, cum ex illa mi-
serabili captiuitate per nostram ecclesiam liberarentur,
a quadam puella quaererem, quomodo fuerit man-
gonibus uendita, raptam se dixit fuisse de domo
parentum suorum; deinde quaesiui utrum ibi sola fuisset inuenta; respondit praesentibus suis parentibus et
fratribus factum. Aderat et frater eius, qui uenerat ad
eam recipiendam et, quia illa parua erat, ipse nobis
quomodo factum esset aperuit. Nocte enim dixit huiusmodi irruisse praedones, a quibus magis se quomodo
poterant occultarent quam eis resistere auderent, bar-
baros esse credentes.

Mercatores autem si non essent, illa non fierent. Nec
sane arbitror hoc Africae malum etiam illic ubi estis
famam tacere; quod incomparabiliter longe minus fuit,
quando tamen imperator Honorius ad praefectum
Hadrianum legem dedit huiusmodi cohibens mercatu-
ras talisque impietatis negotiatores plumbo coercendos
et proscribendos et in exilium perpetuum censuit esse
mittendos; nec de his loquitur in ea lege qui seductos
depraedatos emunt liberos, quod paene solum isti faci-
unt, sed generaliter de omnibus qui uendendas familias
transferunt in prouincias transmarinas. . . .

Immo uero satis dici non potest quam multi in eundem nefarium quaestum mira caecitate cupiditatis et
nescio qua huius uelut morbi contagione defluxerint.
Quis credit inuentam esse mulierem—et hoc apud nos

happened, if indeed the rumor is true. This much I know: I made a personal inquiry to a young girl who was among those who were liberated by our church from a terrible imprisonment. I asked her how she came to be sold to these traffickers, and she told me that she was captured from her parents' house. I asked if she was alone when they came, and she told me that her parents and brother were there. I spoke with her brother as well, because he had come to take her back. Since the sister was so young, he revealed how it all happened. He said that one night these plunderers broke in. They thought that they were barbarians, and so they tried to hide from them rather than resisting.

If there were no dealers, these things would not happen. And I don't think that news about this evil of Africa is unknown where you are. Without a doubt this was a much smaller problem when Emperor Honorius sent a law to the prefect Hadrian to suppress this type of trafficking. He decreed that these disgraceful traffickers be scourged with a leaden ball, lose their property, and be exiled for life. That law is not concerned with those who snatch and pillage free people, which is pretty much all these traffickers do, but is generally concerned with dealers who transport and sell families across the sea. . . .

In truth, it is impossible to tell how many, blinded by greed as if by a contagious disease, have flocked into this despicable trade. If you can believe it, there was a woman right here in Hippo who, pretending to be interested in

apud Hipponem—quae Giddabenses feminas uelut lignorum emendorum causa seducere, includere, affligere soleret et uendere? Quis credat ecclesiae nostrae colonum satis idoneum uxorem suam eandemque matrem filiorum suorum nulla culpa eius offensum solo excitatum feruore huius pestilentiae uendidisse? Adolescens quidam uiginti ferme annorum, calculator notarius cordatus de monasterio nostro est seductus et uenditus, qui uix per ecclesiam potuit liberari.

Si uelim quae nos tantum experti sumus enumerare talia scelera, nullo modo possum. Unum accipe documentum, unde cuncta conicias quae per Africam totam et per omnia eius litora perpetrentur. Ante quattuor fere menses quam ista scriberem de diuersis terris et maxime de Numidia congregati a Galatis mercatoribus—hi enim uel soli uel maxime his quaestibus inhianter incumbunt—ut a litore Hipponiensi transportarentur, adducti sunt. Non defuit fidelis morem nostrum in elemosynis huiusmodi sciens, qui hoc nuntiaret ecclesiae; continuo partim de naui, in qua fuerant impositi, partim de loco ubi occultati fuerant imponendi a nostris—me quidem absente—centum ferme et uiginti homines liberati sunt, in quibus uix quinque aut sex inuenti sunt a parentibus uenditi; ceterorum autem uarios casus, quibus per seductores atque praedones ad Galatas peruenerunt, uix ullus audiens a lacrimis temperat.

buying wood, used to lure other women from Gidda; then she locked them up, beat them, and sold them. Can you believe that a farmer in our church, a respectable guy, sold his wife, the mother of his children, who had done nothing wrong, just because he was stirred by this raging pestilence? Someone about twenty years old, a smart boy who worked as an accountant and secretary, was dragged out of a monastery and sold; we barely managed to save him through our church.

Even if I wanted to, there is no way I could list all the crimes of this sort that I personally witnessed. Take this episode as an example, and gather from it what is happening throughout all of Africa and all its coastland. About four months ago, people from different regions, and especially from Numidia, were gathered by Galatian traffickers to be shipped away from the coast around Hippo. Indeed, it is especially, if not uniquely, Galatians who eagerly devote themselves to these dealings. There happened to be a Christian who knew what we usually do to help in situations like these, and he brought the news to the church. Right away, our people (I was not there) freed them, partly from the ship where they had been boarded and partly from the place where they had been hidden to be boarded. I am talking about 120 people, and it turned out that only five or six among them had been legally sold by their parents. Barely anyone could refrain from tears upon hearing the various vicissitudes of others, how they were misled and seized before they came to the Galatians.

ACKNOWLEDGMENTS

I am grateful to all those who supported me while I worked on this book. I wish to thank Michael Fontaine, for his friendship and encouragement in recommending the Ancient Wisdom for Modern Readers series; Bert Lott and John Bodel for sharing their expertise with ancient inscriptions; Rachel Edney and Bramwell Atkins for assisting me with my research; and Rob Tempio, Mark Bellis, and the entire PUP team for their prompt and always cheerful assistance. I am particularly grateful to my family, and I wish to dedicate this book to my older daughter, Leighanna, with much dear paternal love.

GLOSSARY

aerarium: Roman treasury

amphitheater: "all-around theater," oval-shaped building for spectacles, including gladiatorial combats

Annales: work of history by Tacitus

as (*pl.* asses): Roman bronze coin; starting from 133 BCE, 16 asses correspond to a denarius (originally a denarius corresponded to 10 asses); a cheap loaf of bread would cost about 2 asses

atriensis (*pl.* atrienses; from *atrium*, "entrance room"): steward managing a villa for a landowner

Augustine (354–430 CE): a bishop of Hippo (modern Algeria) and Christian philosopher

Augustus (63 BCE–14 CE): a Roman emperor, author of the *Res gestae* (*Personal Achievements*)

Bok, Francis: a twentieth-century man who became enslaved as a child and who described his experience in *Escape from Slavery: The True Story of My Ten Years in Captivity and My Journey to Freedom in America*

Book of Spectacles (*Liber de spectaculis*): collection of thirty-three epigrams by Martial celebrating the inauguration of the Colosseum in 80 CE

Caelius (ca. 82–47 BCE): a politician; friend of Cicero

Caesar, Julius (100–44 BCE): a successful general, entertainer, and politician

Cassius Longinus, Gaius (ca. 88–42 BCE): an official under Crassus and a murderer of Caesar

catasta: platform for selling slaves

Cato, Elder (234–149 BCE): a consul, censor, and farmer; author of *On Agriculture* (*De agricultura*)

Catullus (ca. 85–54 BCE): a Roman poet

cavea: sitting area in Roman theaters and amphitheaters

cella: small room, used to store wine, or by prostitutes to receive clients

Cestus: an enslaved secretary commemorated in an epitaph

Cicero, Marcus (106–43 BCE): a consul, governor, orator, lawyer, and writer

Cicero, Quintus (102–43 BCE): a governor; brother of Marcus

Cincinnatus, Lucius Quintus (fifth century BCE): a consul, dictator, and farmer; icon of Roman virtue

Codex: twelve-volume collection of Roman laws organized thematically

colonus (*pl.* coloni): tenant renting land and working it for a fee

Colosseum: the most famous and largest amphitheater, inaugurated in 80 CE

Colossus: massive statue built by Nero, of himself, from which the Colosseum, by its proximity to the statue, took its name

Columella (ca. 4–70 CE): the author of *On Agrarian Matters* (*De re rustica*)

Controversiae: work by Elder Seneca, comprising fictitious debates

GLOSSARY

Crassus, Marcus Licinius (ca. 115–53 BCE): a successful entrepreneur but unsuccessful general

Cresimus, Caius Furius: a successful freedman and farmer

De agricultura: work on agriculture by Elder Cato

Delos: island between modern Greece and Turkey, famous for its slave market

denarius (*pl.* denarii): silver coin corresponding to 16 asses or 4 sestertii; major unit of Roman currency; see introduction to chapter 2

De re rustica: work on agrarian matters by Columella

dictata: offensive and defensive moves practiced by gladiators

dies operis: "day of the work," i.e., completion deadline

dies pecuniae: "day of the money," i.e., payment date

Digesta (from *digestum*, "abstract"): fifty-volume selection of legal writings on controversial issues

Douglass, Frederick: a nineteenth-century freedman who had been born into slavery and who described his experience in *Narrative of the Life of Frederick Douglass, an American Slave*

edictum (*pl.* edicta): edict passed by Roman magistrates

editor (*pl.* editores): sponsor of gladiatorial games

epitaph: tombstone inscription

Equiano, Olaudah (ca. 1745–97): a man who became enslaved as a child and who described his experience, including that of a slave market, in *The Life of Olaudah Equiano, or Gustavus Vassa, the African*

familia gladiatoria: team of gladiators from the same ludus

felix: fruitful and lucky

Fortunata: wife of Trimalchio; fictitious character representing a self-made woman in Petronius's *Satyricon*.

Gaius: a prominent Roman jurist

gregarius (*pl.* gregarii): herd gladiators, i.e., those who fought in groups

Hippocrates: a good supervisor commemorated by rural slaves

hordearius (*pl.* hordearii): "barley (hordeum) man," i.e., gladiator

Hortensius (114–50 BCE): a consul, orator, and lawyer; defended Verres against Cicero

infames: individuals labeled with infamia

infamia: "dishonor"; label for people of ill repute, restricting their rights

Institutiones: three-volume introduction to the Roman laws collected in the *Digesta*

insula (*pl.* insulae): apartment building, often crowded, dirty, and dangerous

insularius (*pl.* insularii): apartment renter

iugula: "cut his throat open"; shouted by spectators of gladiatorial combats

Justinian (482–565 CE): emperor of the Eastern Roman Empire; organized Roman law

Juvenal (first to second century CE): a Roman poet, author of *Satires*

laetus: fertile and joyful

lanista (*pl.* lanistae): manager of a gladiatorial ludus

lena (*pl.* lenae): female pimp (owner or manager of prostitutes) leno (*pl.* lenones): male pimp (owner or manager of prostitutes)

lex (*pl.* leges): law passed by a Roman popular assembly

Liber de spectaculis (*Book of Spectacles*): collection of thirty-three epigrams written by Martial celebrating the inauguration of the Colosseum in 80 CE

Livy (59 BCE–17 CE): a Roman historian, author of the 142-volume *History of Rome from Its Foundation*

ludus (*pl.* ludi): school for training gladiators

lupa: she-wolf, i.e., female prostitute

lupanar (*pl.* lupanaria): brothel

magister (*pl.* magistri): elected head of a societas of investors or trainer of gladiators

manceps: official bidder acting on behalf of a societas of investors

mango (*pl.* mangones): slave trafficker

Marcus Aurelius (121–180 CE): a Roman emperor and philosopher; passed a law regulating the expenses for gladiatorial shows

Martial (ca. 39–104 CE): a poet; author of various books of epigrams, including the *Book of Spectacles*

Megiste: a successful greengrocer; commemorated in an epitaph

meretrix (*pl.* meretrices): "woman who earns," i.e., female prostitute

Merula, Publius Decimius Eros: a successful doctor and freedman from Assisi

Metelli: powerful family; backed Verres

missus: "let him go"; shouted by spectators of gladiatorial combats moneta: epithet of Juno, whose temple bordered the mint ("money" < *moneta*)

Naevoleia: a freedwoman commemorated by an epitaph from Pompeii

Naturalis historia: encyclopedic work in thirty-seven books by Elder Pliny

Nero (37–68 CE): a Roman emperor (54–68 CE); built a massive statue of himself, known as the Colossus, from which the Colosseum, by its proximity to the statue, took its name

ordo equestris: class of knights, or equestrian order

pecunia: money, from *pecus*, "cattle"

periculum: "danger," i.e., investment risk

philoploutía: Greek term meaning "love for money," by which Crassus was ruined

plebiscitum (*pl.* plebiscita): law passed by the council of the plebs

Pliny, Elder (23–79 CE): a polymath; wrote the thirty-seven-volume *Natural History*

Pliny, Younger (61–113 CE): a governor, senator, and writer

Plutarch (ca. 46–119 CE): a Greek philosopher and biographer

Pompey (116–48 BC): a successful general and politician

Postumius, Marcus (second half of the second century BCE): a greedy and dishonest publicanus

probation: inspection (of a contracted work)

probator (*pl.* probatores): inspector

Ptolemy XII (ca. 117–51 BCE): a king of Egypt; borrowed from Rabirius Postumus and Roman publicani

publicanus (*pl.* publicani): tax farmer

GLOSSARY

Rabirius Postumus (mid first century BCE): a prominent banker who (over)landed to Ptolemy and was defended by Cicero in 54 BCE

Res gestae (*Personal Achievements*): work written by Augustus and inscribed on his tomb

Res publica: the "public thing," i.e., the Roman state

Sabines: an Italic people, defeated by Cincinnatus

sagina: fattening feed for animals or food for gladiators

Satyricon: Roman picaresque novel written by Petronius in the age of Nero (ca. 60s CE)

scortum (*pl.* scorta): male or female prostitute

senatus consultum (*pl.* consulta): deliberation taken by the Roman senate

Seneca, Elder (ca. 54 BCE–38 CE): an orator; author of the *Controversiae*; father of Younger Seneca

Seneca, Younger (4 BCE–65 CE): a philosopher and writer; teacher of the emperor Nero

sestertius (*pl.* sestertii): small silver coin (especially in the Republic) or large brass coin (especially in the Empire); corresponding to a quarter of a denarius or to 4 asses

societas: "society," a company of investors, including tax collectors

socius (*pl.* socii): shareholders of a societas

stipendium (*pl.* stipendia): salary; the process of weighing (*pendere*) a wage (*stips*)

Strabo (ca. 64 BCE–23 CE): a Greek historian and geographer

Suetonius (ca. 69–123 CE): a biographer; wrote the *Lives of the Twelve Caesars*

Sulla (138–78 BCE): a dictator; fought a bloody civil war

tabellarius (*pl.* tabellarii): "carrier of tabellae [written tablets]," i.e., messenger

Tacitus (ca. 56–120 CE): a Roman historian; wrote the *Annales*

talent: Greek measure of weight, corresponding to about 60 pounds; one talent corresponded to 60 minae or to 6,000 drachmae. The silver drachma was the main monetary unit for the Greeks and comparable to the Roman denarius

Tiberius (24 BCE–37 CE): Roman emperor (14–37 CE); succeeded Augustus

Titus (39–81 CE): Roman emperor (79–81 CE); inaugurated the Colosseum

tributum (*pl.* tributa): tax

tributum capitis: poll tax

tributum soli: land tax

Trimalchio: husband of Fortunata; fictitious character representing a self-made man in Petronius's *Satyricon*

Tryphaena: an enslaved woman commemorating Cestus, a fellow slave, in an epitaph

vectigal (*pl.* vectigalia): tax on public services provided by the state

verna (*pl.* vernae): individual enslaved since birth

Verres (ca. 119–43 BCE): a corrupted governor of Sicily; incriminated by Cicero in 70 BCE and exiled

Verrine Orations: speeches by Cicero incriminating Verres

vicesima libertatis: tax to be paid for manumitting a slave

NOTES

1. Throughout this book, I provide my own translations of Greek and Latin passages. Unless otherwise indicated, the Greek and Latin texts can be found, with English translations, in the Loeb editions (Cambridge, MA: Harvard University Press). Here, Cicero, *On Duties*, translated by Walter Miller (1913), 266–67.

2. Cicero, *On Duties*, 152–53.

3. *Corpus of Latin Inscriptions* (*Corpus inscriptionum latinarum*), bk. 4, inscriptions 6426, 6428a, 206, and 677.

4. Martial, *Epigrams*, translated by David Shackleton Bailey (1993), vol. 1 (bks. 1–5), 230–31.

5. The epitaph of Claudia, *Corpus of Latin Inscriptions* (*Corpus inscriptionum latinarum*), bk. 1, vol. 2, inscription 1211, is often cited as an example of this formula.

6. Horace, *Odes and Epodes*, translated by Niall Rudd (2004), 272–73 and 276–77.

7. Pliny, *Letters*, translated by Betty Radice (1969), vol. 1 (bks. 1–7), 426–29.

8. Frederick Douglass, *Narrative of the Life of Frederick Douglass, an American Slave* (1845; San Diego: Icon Classics, 2005), 84 and 63.

9. Strabo, *Geography*, bks. 3–5, translated by Horace Leonard Jones (1923), 258–59.

10. Plutarch, *Lives*, vol. 2, translated by Bernadotte Perrin (1914), 366–67.

NOTES

11. Strabo, *Geography*, bks. 13–14, translated by Horace Leonard Jones (1929), 328–29.
12. Olaudah Equiano, *The Life of Olaudah Equiano, or Gustavus Vassa, the African* (1789; New York: Dover, 1999), 35–36.
13. Francis Bok, *Escape from Slavery: The True Story of My Ten Years in Captivity and My Journey to Freedom in America* (2003; New York: St. Martin's Griffin, 2004), 8–11.